SIMPLE SOIRÉES

Seasonal Menus for Sensational Dinner Parties

PEGGY KNICKERBOCKER

Foreword by

DIANE JOHNSON

Photographs by

CHRISTOPHER HIRSHEIMER

STEWART, TABORI & CHANG

NEW YORK

CONTENTS

FOREWORD

Diane Johnson

Anyone who loves giving dinner parties will love Peggy Knickerbocker's new cookbook. I am in that category, loving to give dinners but also always on the lookout for a way of doing it easily, on the theory that it is finally more fun, for guests as well as the hostess, if all is seemingly effortless and delicious—easier said than

done. For awhile I thought I had a perfect system for producing a simple *soirée* in France. Banking on the French mistrust of things English, I would buy the main course from the venerable British provisioner Marks and Spencer, which then had a branch in Paris, and simply heat it up. I reasoned that since French hostesses would never enter Marks and Spencer, no one would have tumbled to their excellent ready-made curries and ragouts.

As to heating things up, after all, my thinking went, French hostesses did the same thing—bought one or two of the courses for their impressive meals, often from the frozen food company Picard, which has its own boutiques all over Paris. I was shocked to discover that the French are very devoted to frozen food. My own innovation was to buy the delicious Indian or Indonesian specialties at Marks, dishes which hardly exist on French menus. Alas, with their instinct for delicious food, the French quickly caught on, and soon the food hall was crowded with my French friends.

Such shortcuts have nothing to do with Peggy Knickerbocker's wonderful cookbook, where, in fact, the reader is meant to do all the courses, in steps neatly laid out by Peggy. Her inspiration is that the whole problem with dinner parties lies in having to do a myriad of things at the last minute, with your guests already there, seated trustfully in the living room while you disappear into the kitchen for endless half-hours at a time. We have all wondered what has happened to a host or hostess who has seemed to vanish, only to emerge looking distraught to hoarsely whisper "*à table*" at last, with an air of catastrophe narrowly averted or not averted.

The brilliant organization Peggy proposes transforms all that. She devises delicious menus and reminds you what to do when and in what order, the day before, the day of, and at the last minute before the guests sit down. At last, a clear, set-down-in-black-and-white plan for what needs doing when. If you have ever remembered at the last second that you haven't carved the carrot roses or unthawed the shrimp, you will appreciate this as much as I do. And another of her insights will, I feel, change my life—her point that many dishes are perfectly delicious at room temperature and thus can be made entirely, earlier in the day. This is a great boon to an expedient, last-minute amateur cook like me.

No doubt conceptions of the simple are apt to vary, and what is simple to Peggy, who delights in cooking, may not seem so simple to really lazy cooks like me. She has no suspicion that some of us will not be infusing ice cream with geraniums, though her encouraging tone has made me plan to try it. She told me that the recipe for home-made vanilla ice cream with geraniums is there for people who want extra credit, so she does suspect that some of us will be buying the ice cream, not making it from scratch. But no matter, for the menu will still be delightful, and all her dishes are within my powers, therefore within the powers of most readers.

I have always heard it said that if you get even one recipe for your permanent reperatory from a new cookbook, it will have earned its place on your shelf. Here is one that was news to me. Why had I never thought of putting the pan of hot water, for custard, into the oven when you turn it on, so it will heat up as the oven does? That simple observation alone is a revelation. And why had no one ever told me that making the hollandaise sauce with clarified butter makes it nearly foolproof? Thus does she encourage the reader into doing those formerly hard things, and with a smile at that.

I have always liked menus. I like to read them, even when there's no prospect of cooking the food. I think lots of people approach cookbooks in this way, as a form of dreamy escape reading, a pleasure in itself.

Happily, this book works as good reading, as well as good cooking, for cooks like me and for the more serious; the recipes are wonderful and the organizational directions are absolutely invaluable. A devotee of Peggy's other cookbooks, I have been looking forward to this one, and have been lucky enough to have been among the friends Peggy has tried out these recipes on. Thus have I happily have had the benefit of Peggy's wonderful cooking and cheerful, seemingly effortless hospitality. The pleasure she takes in cooking is infectious and delightful, and so are the results. I commend this book into the reader's hands confident of its welcome.

INTRODUCTION

Giving Great Dinner Parties

I would rather cook and give dinner parties than almost anything. Of course I do other things, but giving dinner parties allows me to pursue some of the other activities I love, shopping unapologetically, expressing heightened domestic urges such as decorating, socializing, trying new recipes, and cooking indulgently for friends.

I get enormous pleasure from planning, executing, and even going to dinner parties. In fact, if I am feeling a little down, one of the best antidotes I know is to call some friends, invite them over, and start rattling the pots and pans. It's a great way to get together with people I love, or want to get to know better, and it's so satisfying for all involved when someone provides a warm, amiable atmosphere to relax, connect, nourish themselves, and feel free to speak their minds.

I decided to write this book for two reasons. First, I am fascinated by the anatomy of a menu and the manner in which it is presented. The art of creating a memorable menu is not unlike other imaginative pursuits. There's a lively balance among intuition, inspiration, experience, and technique. Each meal has a life of its own and, like any living thing, it has its own shapes and needs.

My devotion to cooking and giving parties involves many good meals, lots of traveling, hanging out in the kitchens of good cooks, and reading the works of people who fully understand the art of the

table: M. F. K. Fisher, Alice Waters, Marion Cunningham, Richard Olney, A. J. Liebling, Paul Bertolli, Mario Batali, and many others. An existence based upon food has shaped my life and made it richer. This brings me to the second reason I decided to write this book: I want to encourage you to gather your friends around your table. I want to show that having people over for dinner, lunch, or even drinks does not necessarily have to be troublesome. It might even be fun and could definitely boost the quality of your life.

While you might not be quite as consumed by cooking for friends as I am, there is no reason you, too, can't have warm, simple, delicious dinner parties. There are no excuses. My kitchen in San Francisco is fifty years old and you will see that there, and in my tiny, yet serviceable kitchen in Paris, I am able to handle just about anything. So it is with the support of this book, its many stunning recipes, and tips for success, that I cheer you on.

I will admit that I am at an advantage. I am fortunate to live in two of the world's most breathtaking cities—San Francisco and Paris. The cultural, culinary,

and environmental landscapes of these two places need to be celebrated, and permeate every aspect of this book. I grew up in San Francisco, but have been ogling markets in Paris ever since I was there in college and later when I returned regularly. I was never able to cook in Paris, however, because I didn't have a kitchen. Having been dedicated to a life centered around the table, and having been a caterer, restaurant owner, cook, and food writer over the years, this was excruciatingly frustrating.

A few years ago, I was lucky enough to be able to buy an apartment on rue Madame situated near my favorite organic market—the Sunday Biologique on Boulevard Raspail. Once I signed the papers, I knew what I wanted to do—give dinner parties. It turned out to be the best way to collect all my friends and social contacts in Paris and give my new life some firm, enthusiastic roots.

Simple soirées is a term I love for its subtle elegance, elasticity, and lack of pretension. In France, parties in the evening (soir) are called soirées. I have taken a little liberty with the term in order to include menus that are not just for dinner. In my book, a soirée can be any festive meal, actually—a romantic dinner for two, a quick pasta after the movies, a pot of beef stew simmering in the fireplace. It may be a garden affair, an outdoor grilling party or picnic, an art opening, or a book publishing party. It might be as boisterous as a political fund-raiser, or as traditional as a family holiday. It could be a meal at the end of a long trip or the beginning of a vacation, or as straightforward as a dinner cooked after work when friends gather on a weeknight.

No one has to give a soirée by the book. Individual choice and expression are what make memorable parties memorable. The menus in this book are meant to guide, not constrain. These menus are thoughtfully designed, but feel free to make substitutions and to use the book as you would any other cookbook, recipe by recipe. Some menus can be shortened successfully—for instance, instead of making potatoes for a certain meal, serve grilled, garlic-rubbed bread instead. If the dessert is too much, substitute fresh fruit.

Of course, a successful soirée is not just about following recipes. For each of the menus I offer a party plan that gives a snapshot of what tasks can be done in advance, on the day of the party, and at the last minute. And most of the recipes in this book can be prepared in advance, leaving a bit of final cooking or reheating just before serving. You'll also find decorating ideas for each soirée. While every dinner party is different, following is a discussion of the key elements to focus on when entertaining.

My Menu for Success

For me cooking is never real trouble. I just do for my friends what I am good at—shopping attentively for the most succulent, local, organic food, creating menus in sync with the seasons, and then cooking them with heart. I always cook what pleases me.

INVITATIONS

- Invite guests by phone, e-mail, or handwritten invitation, giving them at least five days' to a week's notice, if not more.
- Be specific about when dinner will be served.
- Explain the tone of the party—casual, outdoors (bring a sweater), fancy, early evening.

EARLY PLANNING

Give yourself time to enjoy planning for parties. Consider your strategy: think of ways to make the party flow easily that include making you and your guests feel comfortable. If you are confident, unharried, and relaxed, your guests will be, too. Don't leave everything to the frantic last moment.

GETTING THE HOUSE READY

- Clean or have your house cleaned the day before the party.
- If it's cold, build a fire.
- If it's warm, get your outdoor area spruced up.
- Make sure the linens are laundered and pressed.
- Buy lots of candles and position them.
- Have your glasses and dishes sparkling clean.

- Get decorations—flowers, bowls of fruit—in place ahead of time.
- Think about lighting—you want to keep it low and inviting.

DECORATING FOR A PARTY

When entertaining is fun for the host, it is fun for the guests. I love the festive exuberance of preparing for parties—it's a present for my friends. I make my house or apartment a welcoming place with flattering lighting and inviting, comfortable places to settle into. I will have set a handsome table and put flowers or bowls of vegetables or fruit around the rooms. The effort you put into getting the house ready for a party displays a certain confidence in yourself and respect for your guests.

SHOPPING

- Do the shopping early. Sort groceries, wash and store produce. Make sure you have plenty of olive oil, butter, and fresh herbs, spices, and condiments.
- If you are buying meat, go to a butcher so you can discuss the cut and the timing for cooking. I don't recommend buying meat from a supermarket, unless you know where the meat comes from. The same goes for fish and fowl. If you only can get to a supermarket and do not find what you want at the meat counter, ask to speak to the butcher about what you need.
- Go to farmers' markets if you have them in your area. Get the best, local, organic food you possibly

can. Almost all the ingredients in this book can be purchased in mainstream markets, and if not, substitutions are noted. Or use the mail order sources at the end of the book.

ADVANCE FOOD PREPARATION

- It's good to serve a dish or two at room temperature so they can be cooked in advance.
- If your menu includes a baked dessert, make it early in the day, or the day before.
- If you are serving my favorite standby hors d'oeuvre—roasted nuts—prepare them a day or two ahead of time and store them in a jar.
- Wash lettuce, spin it dry, and store it in clean towels in the vegetable bin.
- Prepare salad dressings.
- Cut vegetables, make sauces, marinate meat or fowl.

KEEP IT SIMPLE AND NATURAL

For many of us, the kitchen is the new living room. Entertaining has become informal except in very special cases. I no longer worry, as I did when I was a young bride, that all the silver is polished and that the hand towels in the bathroom are pressed, the way my mother did.

One day just before my friend Daryl's birthday lunch (page 78), I realized that the table looked a little sparse. I went outside, clipped off a few olive branches from the trees street in front of my house, and then arranged them down the middle of the table, with lemons and lavender stuck in here and there. It was stunning, simple, and unexpected.

In autumn, I might buy a colossal pumpkin or squash and use it as a centerpiece, or arrange persimmons in a single layer on a rustic wooden platter, or

fill a large silver bowl with pomegranates. Then I put candles around the room. If I am using votives, I place a little water under the candles for easy removal and cleaning. I often have candles and bouquets of herbs or aromatic flowers in the bathroom.

I look for inspiration in my travels. I love the way hors d'oeuvre are served at French cafés—for example, little silver bowls filled with potato chips, olives, or roasted nuts. It's uncomplicated and leaves room for what is to come.

Ask for Help

If you're having a big party and don't feel you can do everything, don't hesitate to get help.

- For a big cocktail soirée, be sure to hire a bartender, not just a friend who promises to look over the bar and then ends up drunk.
- Hire a valet parker if parking is difficult in your neighborhood and you have invited a lot of people. Ask a friend or local caterer for references.
- Ask a friend, a mate, or older children to help. It is fun to hang out in the kitchen with pals; designate jobs. If you feel uncomfortable about grilling, ask a good griller—but make sure to discuss your plan in advance: exactly how you want the meat or fish to be cooked and the time you want it done. If you know how long it will take, tell the griller that the coals need to be ready at say, 7:00, so that the food will come off at 7:30. That way you can coordinate the cooking of the rest of the meal. Be specific with your friends who are helping you.

The Bar

Set up a bar, no matter how simple, to welcome the guests—they want to know where to get a drink when they arrive. If the party is small, let friends help themselves. Have plenty of ice on hand for chilling wine in a bucket or for drinks and water. Offer a good still or sparkling wine as an aperitif, a bottle of vodka for those who might want a mixed drink, and some cold beer. Have plenty of chilled carbonated water on hand. Consult a good wine merchant if you are uncertain about what to serve with your meal. Count on at least half a bottle of water and half a bottle of wine per person at the table, more if your friends love to drink. Buy the wine a day ahead of time to get whatever needs to be chilled into the refrigerator.

Table Size

The closer people sit, the better the party, I say. I used to put extra leaves in my table to spread my guests out comfortably but then I noticed that in Paris, because space is more limited, parties were warmer and cozier when everyone could join in on the same conversation.

Table Setting

Go all out, use beautiful tablecloths and napkins (what else are they for), set out sparkling glasses, and keep the centerpiece low so that people can see each other across the table. If you are serving family-style, remove the centerpiece and replace it with platters of food once you sit down. Or make a handsome arrangement of fruit in the middle of the table and use it as a dessert course, perhaps with cheese.

Menu Planning

Whether in Paris or San Francisco, I cook every day for family and friends. My travels back and forth have polished an aesthetic that filters through my cooking

and party giving. My recurring fascination is about creating delicately balanced, unforgettable meals. It does not happen passively. I start thinking about the next meal before I finish the one at hand. I give great thought to the menus—the equilibrium at play. For me, planning a menu is almost as gratifying as cooking and eating it.

I have never met anyone as opinionated about menus as Richard Olney, the cook and author who lived in the south of France and wrote a definitive book on the subject (*The French Menu Cookbook*). The prickly Olney had astoundingly clear ideas about menus, feeling that they should be based upon sensuous and aesthetic concepts with interrelationships between the courses so that each course provides contrast to the one preceding it. "The movement through courses should ascend from light and delicate and more complex fla-

vors through progressively richer and more full-bodied flavors," he explained in his book. "The eye," he said, "must be flattered as well as the palate."

For instance, he'd discourage (as I would), serving tomatoes on a red plate or spinach on a green one. He'd never serve a meal made up of all white or all beige components. A first-rate menu should exhibit a variation of flavors, food groups, colors, and textures. You wouldn't want two salads with the same sort of vinaigrette, nor would you want a creamy sauce during the main course and, say, a crème anglaise for dessert. Parsley should not be sprinkled indiscriminately over everything, and in fact I actually feel that most garnishes usually detract rather than add to a dish. You get the picture—think of variety for all the senses.

With drinks, I serve something salty, crunchy, and not filling, say warm roasted nuts or olives or crisp chilled radishes. The main course is inspired by what grabs my attention at the market. It might be a pork tenderloin crusted with a seeded spicy rub from my favorite Parisian butcher or the *Gnafron* that I had in Lyon and for which I sought out the recipe for a year. It always depends on the season, the occasion, and my mood. I usually follow the main course in the French manner, with a crisp salad of seasonal greens or perhaps an escarole or radicchio salad lightly dressed with an anchovy dressing. The salad cleanses the palate and grooms the appetite for a course of carefully chosen cheeses or an easy, elegant dessert. (A composed salad of several elements is best served as a first course.)

GUESTS

I have a great group of friends with whom I cook regularly. We watch Sunday night TV together, share birthdays, and travel together. We feel comfortable together and we help one another at the market and in the kitchen. There is no pressure other than to make a delicious meal every time.

But I also have dinner parties where I am not as familiar with my guests, but want to get to know them. This breeds just the tension I like. The man to woman ratio is hardly significant anymore at my parties; what matters is that the crowd is lively, warm, and interesting.

MAKE YOURSELF AVAILABLE TO BE A GOOD HOST

- Gather people you love or those whom you want to get to know.
- Have children taken care of so they can have fun with the guests or be otherwise amused.
- Don't answer your phone once the guests arrive.

- Don't rush the meal.
- Don't do the dishes while your friends are there; scrape and stack, but being overly concerned about cleanliness detracts from your hosting responsibilities.
- Relax; have a great simple soirée.

SO MANY PEOPLE have shelves filled with cookbooks but still socialize in restaurants. Restaurants certainly have their place, but there is nothing like relaxing in someone's kitchen or at the dinner table for as long as you want, with no pressure to move or to restrain yourself. It is here that you get to feel fully connected. Where else except around a comfortable dinner table, can we give and get so much? We form lasting friendships and solid ideologies at tables where lively conversation and good food flourish.

SPRING
TO THE RESCUE

Fried Squash Blossoms

· · · · ·

Butterflied Leg of Lamb Stuffed with Tapenade

· · · · ·

Roasted Potatoes and Artichokes with
Fava Beans and Peas (Barigoule)

· · · · ·

Lemon Mousse with Fresh Blueberries

Taking full advantage of the seasonal delights of spring, this meal was born out of a visit to the farmers' market in early June—when squash blossoms make their yearly debut, artichokes begin to appear, spring lamb is available, and blueberries make a triumphant return. A leg of lamb makes an ideal celebration dish. I first made this meal when the arrival of a friend from Paris coincided with the appearance of spring lamb at the market, giving me a great excuse for a party.

The squash blossoms are easy to fry, and since they must be eaten immediately, they are an easy hors d'oeuvre to serve just before carving the lamb. A butterflied leg of lamb is striking roasted on a bed of thyme and stuffed with a deep, rich black tapenade, an idea inspired by the late Provençal cook, Richard Olney.

The barigoule (a sautéed mixture of artichokes, potatoes, fava beans, and peas) is a Parisian recipe that covers all the bases, allowing for potatoes and vegetables to be served together in one dish. The lemon mousse is tart and stimulating after the slightly salty tapenade, and so sumptuous in the mouth with the popping blueberries.

PARTY PLAN

DAY OF THE PARTY

- Salt the lamb
- Prepare the tapenade
- Make the lemon mousse
- Prepare the vegetables: shuck the peas and favas

LAST MINUTE

- Trim the artichokes
- Fry the squash blossoms

DECORATING IDEAS

As my friend Niloufer says, "Try to keep the spirit of the season and the mood of the occasion in mind, considering the colors of the food against the plates." So for this spring dinner I arrange sphagnum moss down the center of the table and slip in little clusters of violets and lilies of the valley in small vases.

This sort of meal is ideal for spring holiday celebrations, such as Easter. The moss with the flowers would look cheerful with the addition of pale blue eggs, brown eggs, or even colored eggs set within the moss. Or you can place a huge wooden bowl with a few dozen pure fresh eggs on the table.

FRIED SQUASH BLOSSOMS

¾ cup all-purpose flour

1 cup dry white wine

½ cup cold sparkling water

1 quart olive oil or peanut oil

12 squash blossoms (with or without tiny zucchini attached)

Salt for sprinkling

During those few months when these delicate, lovely blossoms are in the market, buy them and fry them to eat as you sip wine before dinner. When I find blossoms still attached to tiny zucchini, I slit the zucchini in half and dip the whole affair into the batter. For the best results use a deep, heavy pot and have a deep-fat frying thermometer on hand.

In a medium-sized bowl, combine the flour, wine, and water. Whisk until the mixture resembles a thin pancake batter.

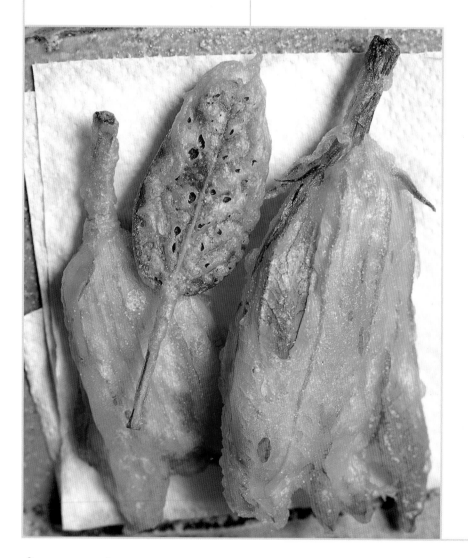

Heat the oil in a deep, heavy pot over high heat to a temperature of 350°F or until just before smoking.

Dip a blossom into the batter, shaking off any excess against the side of the bowl. Drop it gently into the oil allowing it to brown nicely for a few minutes. Using tongs or a slotted spoon, remove the blossom and drain it on paper towels or on a wire rack placed over paper towels.

Repeat with the remaining blossoms, frying no more than 3 at a time. If you crowd the blossoms, they will lower the temperature of the oil and you will not get as crispy results.

Salt the blossoms generously and eat while warm.

SERVES 6 TO 8

Butterflied Leg of Lamb
Stuffed with Tapenade

This boned and bound leg of lamb, roasted on a bed of thyme and stuffed with a black olive tapenade that ends up in the center of each slice, makes a dramatic impact as you remove it from the oven, sizzling and aromatic. The cut slices reveal pinwheels of tapenade. The tapenade can also be spread on toast as an hors d'oeuvre. Ask your butcher to bone and butterfly the lamb, and to remove any tough fibers.

TO MAKE THE TAPENADE

Place the olives, anchovies, capers, garlic, cayenne, and thyme into a mortar or the bowl of a food processor. Pound or pulse until the mixture becomes a coarse puree. Add the olive oil and mix or pulse to combine.

TO PREPARE THE LAMB

Preheat the oven to 450°F.

Open the butterflied lamb on a flat work surface and salt the inside. Spread the tapenade down the center. Have ready about 8 lengths of kitchen twine, long enough to wrap around the meat and tie it in a knot. Roll the meat up lengthwise into a neat package with the ends tucked in. Tie with string every couple of inches, going around the width and then two passes lengthwise. Spread the thyme out in a roasting pan, and place the roast, cut side down, on top. Salt and pepper the exterior generously and drizzle with the olive oil.

Roast the lamb for about 20 minutes and then reduce the heat to 375°F and roast for about 1 hour, until a meat thermometer reads 125° to 135°F at the fattest point (the narrower ends will get done first but the center will be fine as you let it rest for 15 minutes before serving). Carve crosswise into ¾-to 1-inch-thick slices, so you have a pinwheel of black tapenade against the pink meat.

Serve with Mint Sauce (page 186) on the side or just spoon the cooking juices over the meat, along with any tapenade that fell into the pan.

SERVES 6 TO 8
(Makes about 1 cup tapenade)

FOR THE TAPENADE

½ pound large Greek olives, pitted

4 to 6 anchovies (preferably salt-cured), boned, rinsed, and chopped

4 tablespoons capers (preferably salt-cured), soaked, rinsed, and chopped

1 clove garlic, minced with a pinch of salt

Pinch of cayenne

1 tablespoon minced fresh thyme leaves

¼ cup extra-virgin olive oil

FOR THE LAMB

1 leg of lamb, about 6 pounds, butterflied

Kitchen twine

A few bunches of thyme

Salt and freshly ground black pepper

3 tablespoons olive oil

ROASTED POTATOES AND ARTICHOKES WITH FAVA BEANS AND PEAS (Barigoule)

1½ pounds fava beans, shelled

¼ cup extra-virgin olive oil

1 large onion, finely chopped

8 to 10 firm, small potatoes, washed and cut into bite-sized pieces

1 pound small artichokes, trimmed, turned, and thinly sliced (see sidebar)

Splash of dry white wine

1 pound English peas, shelled

Salt and freshly ground black pepper

¼ cup chopped parsley

2 cloves garlic, minced

I noticed on several spring menus in Parisian restaurants that the term barigoule was used for dishes such as this. The Larousse Gastronomique says that barigoule refers to a mushroom from the south of France or to artichokes stuffed with that mushroom. Parisian chefs seem to have taken liberty with the name and because I love the name, I will too. To me it is a handsome and delicious toss of potatoes, artichokes, favas, and peas. It is a starch and green vegetable all in one dish. This makes a good party dish because it can be prepared in advance and reheated.

Bring a small pot of salted water to a boil. Add the shelled fava beans and boil for 1 minute. Drain, and plunge the beans into ice water to stop the cooking and to keep them bright green. Drain again, then slip the skin off each fava bean with your fingers.

Warm 2 tablespoons of the olive oil in a large skillet over medium-high heat. Add the onions and cook until they release their fragrance, about 2 minutes. Add the potatoes and cook, stirring until they become tender when pierced with a fork, 8 to 10 minutes.

Meanwhile, in another skillet, heat the remaining 2 tablespoons olive oil, and cook the artichokes for 20 to 30 minutes over low heat until nicely brown and tender. Add a splash of white wine or a little more olive oil as needed. Add the potatoes to the artichoke skillet and fold in the fava beans and peas. Sprinkle with salt and pepper. Transfer the mixture to a gratin dish and serve. (If you prepare the dish in advance, warm it in a 400°F oven for about 5 to 7 minutes before serving.)

SERVES 6

Preparing Baby Artichokes

Remove at least three to four layers of outer leaves to reach the light green interior leaves. Working with one artichoke at a time, trim off the dark spot where the artichoke was attached to the bush and the top 1 inch of the leaves. Cut the trimmed artichoke in half lengthwise, and lay flat side down. Using a very sharp knife, slice the artichoke lengthwise as thinly as possible.

Lemon Mousse with Fresh Blueberries

Here's a classic French dessert that is a great party choice, as it can be made in advance. The combination of the mousse and ripe blueberries speaks to the joy of early spring.

Scatter the blueberries on a clean kitchen towel so they are very dry.

Fill a medium saucepan one-third to one-half full with water and bring to a gentle simmer. Whisk together the egg yolks, sugar, lemon juice, and lemon zest in a metal bowl that will fit over the saucepan. Set the bowl in the saucepan and stir or whisk continuously until the mixture starts to thicken. Remove from the heat and let cool.

In a large bowl, beat the egg whites to soft peaks and set aside. In another bowl, beat the cream to stiff, but not dry, peaks and set aside.

Gently fold the whipped cream into the cooled egg yolk mixture, until well incorporated. Then fold that mixture into the egg whites until well incorporated. Cover the mousse with plastic wrap and refrigerate until chilled and ready to serve, at least 1 hour.

Divide the mousse among 6 to 8 dessert bowls and scatter the blueberries on top.

SERVES 6 TO 8

3 pints fresh blueberries, sorted, rinsed in cold water

8 large egg yolks (reserve 4 whites for use later)

1 cup sugar

¾ cup fresh lemon juice

2 tablespoons grated lemon zest

1 cup whipping cream

In Love with Gnafron

Assorted Dried Sausages

· · · · ·

Gnafron

· · · · ·

Red and Green Salad

· · · · ·

Rhubarb and Strawberry Compote

· · · · ·

Demitasse Tray

Since my goal in writing this book is to get people to cook and invite friends over, sometimes having just one stellar dish is all that is required.

The sole reason for this meal is to make and serve one of my favorite dishes, *Gnafron*, which is an andouille flan wrapped in cabbage leaves, steamed to wobbly perfection, and drizzled with garlic cream. It is remarkable in the sense that your guests have never had anything like it— it looks beautiful and tastes densely divine and delicious.

Gnafron provides simplicity and a certain ease, as it can be made before the guests arrive, then cooked or reheated at the last minute. Prepare *Gnafron* for adventuresome guests and for a supper rather than a big meal. I make this on Sunday evenings when I feel like seeing my friends informally, perhaps before Sunday night TV or a movie.

For hors d'oeuvre, the menu includes another specialty of Lyon, a variety of sausages, served on a small wooden board. Serve chilled radishes alongside, or a bowl of olives. The crisp red and green salad offers a clean pause to the meal. In keeping with our quest for simplicity, a rosy compote pairs rhubarb with its ideal partner—strawberries.

There is something so French about using trays. Set up a tray with six demitasses or small glasses, small spoons, a bowl of brown sugar cubes, and a plate with dark chocolate squares or other candies. When dessert is finished, make espresso and decaf and bring it to the table on the tray.

PARTY PLAN

DAY OF THE PARTY

- Prepare the Gnafron for baking
- Make the garlic cream
- Wash the salad greens
- Make the salad dressing
- Set up the dessert so it can be cooked at the last minute, or make in advance and reheat just before serving.
- Set up a tray for after-dinner coffee or tea

DECORATING IDEAS

If possible, go to your farmers' market or produce market and buy a big, beautiful, dramatic cabbage. Place it in the middle of the table. It is in keeping with the Lyonnaise inspiration for the meal.

GNAFRON

FOR THE GNAFRON

2 tablespoons extra-virgin olive oil

2 tablespoons unsalted butter

1 carrot, diced

½ pound andouille sausage or other distinctively flavored, spicy sausage, finely chopped

1 medium onion, minced

2 teaspoons fresh thyme leaves or 1 teaspoon dried thyme

1 bay leaf

Salt and freshly ground black pepper

Splash of white wine

1 Napa cabbage, separated, tough parts of the core removed (16 to 20 leaves)

2 tablespoons unsalted butter for greasing the ramekins

4 large eggs

¼ cup heavy cream

FOR THE GARLIC CREAM

3 cloves garlic

Pinch of sugar

Pinch of salt

Splash of white wine

½ cup heavy cream

This surprising dish is a light, speckled flan typically made with andouille sausage, which is wrapped in a napa cabbage leaf, and served with garlic cream. Gnafron is custardy perfection. The flavor is assertive but softened by the warm garlic cream that pools around it. If you are not a fan of andouille (or cannot find the real thing where you live), use another spicy sausage or a well-seasoned Italian sausage.

TO MAKE THE GNAFRON

In a heavy saucepan, melt the butter in the olive oil. Add the carrot, sausage, onion, thyme, and bay leaf. Season with salt and pepper to taste. Simmer slowly for 15 minutes. When the mixture becomes slightly dry, add the wine and stir well.

When the ingredients have become soft and aromatic, another 5 to 10 minutes, remove the pan from the heat and allow the mixture to cool for about 10 minutes.

Meanwhile, in a large skillet, bring 4 cups of salted water to a simmer over high heat. Blanch the cabbage leaves (tender parts only), a few at a time. Remove with tongs and allow them to drain on clean kitchen towels.

Grease 6 small ramekins or soufflé dishes with butter. Line the dishes with the cabbage leaves, allowing them to overlap so that when the sausage mixture is spooned onto them, they can be folded over to make a little package.

In a medium-sized bowl, beat the eggs with the cream, and salt and pepper to taste. Stir the sausage mixture into the egg mixture and mix well. Divide the mixture among the lined ramekins and fold the overlapping leaves over the top. Don't worry if the mixture leaks out around the leaves.

Preheat the oven to 350°F.

Place the ramekins in a deep baking pan large enough to hold them all. Pour warm water around them so that it comes ¾ of the way up the sides. Place the pan in the oven and bake for about 1 hour, or until the Gnafron has set and the top is firm to the touch. If the tops begin to brown or get too dark, place a sheet of foil over the tops. It's okay if the tops get golden brown.

(Continued)

While the *Gnafron* bakes, make the garlic cream. In a small heavy pot, combine the garlic, sugar, salt, and a splash of water; cook over medium-low heat for about 2 minutes. Add a splash of white wine, allow it to cook down for 3 to 5 minutes. Reduce the heat to low, add the cream, and warm it for about 3 minutes. Turn the heat off and allow the garlic to steep in the cream until the *Gnafron* comes out of the oven. Reheat the garlic cream over low heat, the cream with be slightly thin. Remove and discard the garlic.

To serve, run a knife around the sides of the ramekins to loosen the mixture. Turn out onto a platter or individual plates or serve in the ramekins. Serve with a little garlic cream drizzled over the tops.

SERVES 6

In Love with Gnafron

It's just like love. I find a dish that besots me and I am a woman obsessed. It becomes the only food that can sustain me and the only thing I want to master. I Google it, I write to food historians to learn of its lineage, I consult cookbooks for technique, and, if confusion lingers I plead with chefs for help as I would a therapist. But when I fell in love with Gnafron it was as if I had fallen for someone on a one-night stand, never to be seen again.

It started one wintry day a few years ago when a Parisian friend, his dog Arturo, and I took a train from Paris to Lyon for lunch. Hunger had started to scratch at our stomachs as we wandered through an open-air market on a quay on the Rhone seeking advice about a restaurant. We found a good prospect—a pleasantly plump sausage maker—and asked her where she liked to lunch.

The nice woman sent us to the Rue des Marronniers, where she assured us all of the restaurants were good. We ended up at Chabert et Fils just as it was about to close. Arturo nestled himself at our feet and, after hearing the description of Gnafron, I quickly ordered it. And once the flan, wrapped in pale green leaves, was placed before me, I knew it would be worth the trip. After one bite, I was smitten. I asked to speak to the chef but she had departed. Crestfallen, I picked up her card so I could get the scoop later. I could not get Gnafron out of my mind. It was smooth and a bit mysterious, obscured as it was beneath the cabbage leaves, its assertiveness softened by the garlic cream.

It took me more than a year to run the recipe down. All I uncovered about mysterious Gnafron was that it shared its name with a hard-drinking yet philosophical character in a children's puppet show, Guignol, written by Laurent Mourquet in the 1880s. Then I ran into an old friend at a party who told me that her fiancé lived in Lyon. I asked for help. As it turned out, he lived just blocks from the restaurant and he sent me the recipe scribbled in French on a cocktail napkin. My version of Gnafron has become part of my repertoire, an all-occasion treat I serve at luncheon parties and suppers by the fire.

RED AND GREEN SALAD

I had this colorful crunchy salad at Greens Restaurant in San Francisco. Annie Sommerville, the chef, had scattered a handful of slightly salty pistachios on top. It is ever so psychedelic in its colorful crispness. Treviso is the elongated red and white type of radicchio. The round version Rossa Chiogia is fine, too.

Wash and spin dry the lettuce leaves, then chill them while you make the dressing.

In a small bowl whisk together the vinegar, salt and pepper to taste, garlic, and mustard. Continue whisking while drizzling in the oil. Toss the leaves with the dressing in a salad bowl and scatter the pistachios on top.

SERVES 4 TO 6

1 head romaine lettuce

2 heads Treviso radicchio

2 tablespoons red wine vinegar

Salt and freshly ground black pepper

1 clove garlic, minced

1 teaspoon Dijon mustard

⅓ cup pistachio oil, or extra-virgin olive oil

A handful of toasted and salted pistachios

RHUBARB AND STRAWBERRY COMPOTE

The dessert at one of my first restaurant meals as a young student in Paris was a large tureen of a bracing pink stew of rhubarb and strawberries. I was amazed that the waiter put the tureen on the table and let me help myself. I ate and ate until my French "mother" told me it was impolite to take more than one serving. I love this dessert after a rich meal and now I can have as many servings as I like.

Rinse the rhubarb stalks and trim the ends. Peel off any stringy parts with a vegetable peeler and cut the stalks into 1-inch lengths. Place the rhubarb in a heavy pan with the sugar, lemon zest, and lemon juice. Cook slowly over low heat, stirring constantly, until the rhubarb is tender and the liquid has thickened, 10 to 15 minutes. Remove from the heat. Stir in the strawberries, sweeten with more sugar if necessary.

Pour into a tureen and serve at the table in dessert glasses or compote cups, with a little ice cream or crème fraîche on top.

SERVES 4 TO 6

2 pounds rhubarb

¾ cup sugar

Grated zest of one lemon

Juice of one lemon

1 pint strawberries, hulled and halved

Vanilla ice cream or crème fraîche

A Mexican Fiesta

Margaritas

· · · · ·

Toasted Pumpkin Seeds

· · · · ·

Seviche of Bay Scallops

· · · · ·

Authentic Guacamole

· · · · ·

Salpicon

· · · · ·

Warm Tortillas

· · · · ·

Black Beans with Epazote

· · · · ·

Rum-Banana Bake

This splashy party with its vivid menu could easily be used for a Cinco de Mayo celebration or for a festive gathering of friends who like assertively seasoned food. While the menu is broad, it is straightforward and easy, especially if started a day in advance.

Feel free to use only as many recipes as you like. But the intent here is that the flavors of each dish will build on those that precede it. The saltiness of the margaritas and pumpkin seeds make you long for a scoop of creamy, spicy guacamole. The seviche is slightly sweet but delivers a gloved punch. Guests enjoy piling the black beans and *salpicon*—the delicious, slow-cooked, slightly pickled, shredded beef salad—into warm tortillas. The meal ends with a doubly sweet dessert of bananas, dark rum, and brown sugar.

A little advance work does the trick towards making this soirée simple. *Salpicon* is best made the day before, allowing the flavors to intensify as they mingle. The beans must be soaked and simmered in advance, but that takes no effort at all. Roasting the pumpkin seeds and squeezing the lime juice ahead of time give you a head start so that when friends arrive, the bulk of the work is done and you can have fun making the other dishes as time allows.

PARTY PLAN

When I serve a meal such as this, most of the fun happens in the kitchen. I invite friends over in the late afternoon to have margaritas or beer and help cook. I prepare the salpicon and the beans ahead of time and usually roast the pumpkin seeds myself, then I give the remaining recipes to the guests. Even if they are not particularly good cooks, they all get to feel as if they have contributed to the meal.

THE DAY BEFORE

- Buy plenty of Mexican beer and a bottle of tequila. Stock up on lots and lots of limes; they go with everything in this menu—drinks and food. The Mexican stores in my city sell limes inexpensively—you could use up to three dozen limes.

- Toast the pumpkin seeds

- Soak the beans

- Squeeze the lime juice for seviche and margaritas

- Cook and marinate the brisket

DAY OF THE PARTY

- Cook the beans

- Chop the herbs—cilantro, parsley, and epazote

- Chop the chiles for seviche, guacamole, and salpicon

Decorating Ideas

In front of your house, welcome your guests with luminarias, the traditional Mexican lanterns consisting of paper bags filled with sand with a candle in them. The flame shimmers through the bag.

Spread a bright tablecloth with multicolored napkins—red, yellow, green, blue, hot pink, orange. I have a collection of hand-carved figures from Oaxaca that I place on the table around votive candles. Then I scatter dried red chiles around them. Use bright-colored platters or ones that contrast nicely with each dish: an orange bowl for the guacamole, a white platter for the salpicon so that the color of the brown meat does not get muddled, and so on.

Cut short bunches of sunflowers (about four inches from the flower) and put them in small, round, clear glass vases to go on the table. That way you get a lot of color and the arrangements are low enough so that your guests can see one another across the table. Light other bright multicolored candles and put them around the house.

A large bowl of limes looks handsome as a kitchen table decoration, too.

- Chop the onions and zest the orange for the seviche
- Chop the green onions, tomato, jalapeño, and cilantro for the guacamole

LAST MINUTE

- Prepare the seviche
- Make the guacamole
- Make the margaritas
- Decorate the salpicon with avocados, tomatoes, and romaine leaves
- Warm the beans and sprinkle with queso fresco
- Warm the tortillas
- Assemble the dessert to put in the oven as dinner is served

MARGARITAS

Mix these frosty drinks in batches on the spot in the blender. Margaritas are traditionally served as a cocktail and not with the meal; they are a strong before-dinner drink. Buy the small Mexican limes or limons, if you can find them, as their flavor is great.

Rub the rim of each glass with a wedge of lime and dip the rim into a saucer filled with margarita salt or kosher salt.

Place the ingredients in a blender and blend until the ice cubes have broken and the mix is frothy. Pour into the prepared glasses. If you do not have a blender that crushes the ices, add a little water to the drink and serve with ice cubes.

SERVES 2

Margarita salt or kosher salt

2 ounces tequila

2 ounces fresh lime juice

1 ounce Cointreau

10 ice cubes

TOASTED PUMPKIN SEEDS

A big bowl of warm and salty toasted pumpkin seeds is inviting and not too filling when you have a Mexican meal to follow. They go well with margaritas, too. They can be briefly reheated or served at room temperature.

Heat a large, well-seasoned or nonstick skillet over medium-high heat.

Place the pumpkin seeds in a colander in the sink, and add a splash of water, so the salt will adhere. Sprinkle on the salt and toss well. Toast the pumpkin seeds in the skillet in batches one layer deep, stirring or shaking the pan constantly until they begin to pop and become barely golden. Do not let them brown or they will be bitter.

Pour the seeds into a bowl. Toss with the oil when they are still warm. Taste to make sure they are salty enough, if not, add more. Serve warm or at room temperature. Store in an airtight container for up to 3 days.

SERVES 8 TO 10

1 pound raw hulled green pumpkin seeds

1 tablespoon salt

1 teaspoon extra-virgin olive oil

SEVICHE OF BAY SCALLOPS

1 pound day boat sea scallops, fresh bay scallops, or red snapper

Zest of 1 lime, minced

Zest of half an orange, minced

3 green onions, sliced in thin rounds, (white part and the crisp section of the green part)

¼ cup chopped flat-leaf parsley

¼ cup chopped cilantro leaves

1 tablespoon dried oregano, preferably Mexican

1 teaspoon minced jalapeño pepper (more if you prefer heat)

Salt

Pinch of crushed red pepper flakes, optional

⅓ cup fresh lime juice (about 3 juicy limes)

Since the scallops "cook" in the lime juice and are not cooked with heat, it is very important that they be impeccably fresh. The term "day boat scallops" refers to scallops that have been caught in a boat that just goes out for the day—in other words, the catch has not been frozen. You can also make this dish with pristinely fresh red snapper.

If the scallops are large, cut them into nickel-sized pieces, or if using bay scallops, leave them whole. (If you are using snapper, use needle-nose pliers to pull out any bones that you can feel by running your finger along the fillets. Cut the fillets into nickel-sized pieces.) Place the fish in a shallow, nonreactive ceramic or glass dish, so they will "cook" uniformly.

A few hours before serving, sprinkle all of the remaining ingredients, except the lime juice, evenly over the top of the scallops and refrigerate. About 30 minutes before you are ready to serve, pour the lime juice over the scallops, toss gently, and allow them to "cook" in the refrigerator, turning them once or twice to make sure all sides get the lime treatment. Do not marinate for too long or they will become, "overcooked" and mushy.

Taste the fish and add more salt if you feel it is necessary.

Serve in a large, pretty seashell or an earthenware dish and provide small forks or short skewers for eating.

SERVES ABOUT 8 AS AN HORS D'OEUVRE OR SIDE DISH

Authentic Guacamole

Everyone loves guacamole, and I like to keep it simple. Salt is a very important ingredient in this dish, but I once made it too salty and added a pinch of brown sugar to counteract the saltiness. It brings out the flavor of the other ingredients and its sweetness was imperceptible. Now I always include a pinch of brown sugar. The amount of salt, pepper, and lime juice used is up to you. Mash the mixture with your hands so that you can make sure most of the avocado lumps are broken down, leaving some in for texture.

Place all of the ingredients in an earthenware or glass bowl and mix well with your hands, leaving some chunks. Fold into a serving bowl, surrounded by good thick tortilla chips.

SERVES 8 TO 10

6 to 8 ripe black-skinned Hass avocados, peeled with seed removed

8 green onions (white part and firm section of green part), finely chopped

1 cup chopped cilantro leaves

1 medium-sized tomato, seeded, and chopped

1 or 2 jalapeño chiles, slit lengthwise, seeded, and minced

A pinch of brown sugar

Salt and freshly ground black pepper

Juice of 1 or 2 limes

Tortilla chips

SALPICON

FOR THE BRISKET

2 tablespoons extra-virgin olive oil

Salt

4 to 6 pounds boneless brisket of beef, most of the fat removed

2 large white onions, thinly sliced

1 bay leaf

1 tablespoon dried oregano, preferably Mexican

FOR THE DRESSING

One 7-ounce can chipotle chiles en adobo

½ cup extra-virgin olive oil

⅓ cup fresh lime juice

¼ cup white wine vinegar

Salt

3 cloves garlic, minced

1 medium red onion, diced

¾ cup finely chopped fresh cilantro leaves

FOR SERVING

3 medium-ripe tomatoes, cut into wedges

2 avocados, cut into wedges

2 heads romaine lettuce, washed and separated into leaves, tough outer leaves discarded

1 bunch radishes, trimmed and cut into thin slices, chilled in ice water, and drained

When I visited El Paso to write a story for Saveur magazine on border food, Park Kerr, owner of The El Paso Chile Company, made a version of this dish one night for a party. This shredded beef salad has outstanding flavor, and can be eaten with romaine leaves or piled into warm tortillas.

Salpicon is a great choice for a party as it is made ahead of time. It takes about 6 hours to make (during 4 to 5 of them the meat cooks on its own). If you give yourself plenty of time, it is very simple and definitely worth the effort.

TO PREPARE THE BRISKET

Place a deep, large, heavy skillet over medium-high heat. When the pan is hot add the olive oil. Salt the brisket liberally then brown it for 7 to 10 minutes on each side.

Add the onions to the skillet. Lower the heat to medium and add enough water to cover the meat. Add the bay leaf and oregano and stir well to combine. Simmer gently for 4 to 6 hours (depending upon the thickness and tenderness of the meat), until the brisket is very tender, turning it midway through the cooking time. The meat is done when it shreds easily when coaxed with a fork. (NOTE: If the ends of the brisket are not as wide as the center, they will cook more quickly. Transfer the brisket to a cutting board after about 3½ hours and, if they seem done and easy to shred, slice off the end pieces. Place the center cut back into the braising liquid and continue to cook until the meat can be easily shredded with a fork. Set the ends aside.)

When the brisket is done, remove it from the pan and place it on a cutting board with a lip, so the juices will not run off. Let it cool for about 30 minutes, then remove any remaining large amounts of fat and discard. Shred the meat (including the end pieces if removed from the cooking liquid earlier) with two forks or your fingers. Cut the shreds into 1-inch-long strips. Place the meat in a large bowl and set aside.

Drain the chipotles, reserving the adobo sauce in the can. Seed (as best you can) and chop the chipotles and mix them with the oil, lime juice, vinegar, salt to taste, and garlic. Taste the dressing. If it is not spicy enough, add a little of the reserved adobo sauce.

Fold three quarters of this mixture into the shredded beef. The *salpicon* should not be dry, but it should not be swimming in the dressing, either. If you think the remaining dressing is necessary, add it now. Stir in the onions and cilantro. (The dish can be made up to a day ahead of time up to this point and refrigerated.)

Thirty minutes before serving, take the *salpicon* out of the refrigerator, taste for seasoning, and gently stir in the tomatoes and the avocados. Arrange the *salpicon* on a large white platter lined with a bed of crisp romaine leaves. Scatter the radishes over the top.

SERVES 8 TO 10

WARM TORTILLAS

Line a basket with linen napkins. Wrap a handful of flour or corn tortillas in aluminum foil or a clean kitchen towel and place them in a 300°F oven for 5 to 7 minutes. Or you can heat the tortillas in a hot cast iron skillet, a *comal*, or over an open fire, one by one, and place them in the basket and cover them, as they are done. Serve the basket of tortillas on the table. Plan on 3 tortillas per person.

BLACK BEANS WITH EPAZOTE

1 pound black beans

1 small white onion studded with
2 cloves

3 to 5 sprigs fresh epazote leaves or
1 teaspoon dried, optional

1 tablespoon salt, or more to taste

⅓ cup crumbled queso fresco or
grated Monterey Jack

These beans are pure and delicious, and uncomplicatedly elegant. Epazote leaves (a few small sprigs) offer a delicate, herbaceous flavor. Or you can just serve the beans with a little crumbled queso fresco or grated Monterey Jack on top. You can make the beans a day ahead of time, refrigerate them, and bring them back to room temperature before reheating. Be sure there is enough liquid or extra water in the pan when you reheat them so they don't burn.

TIP: Buy the beans from a store where there is frequent turnover so their freshness will be assured. The older the beans, the longer they will take to cook.

Pick through the beans, discarding any tiny stones, then rinse the beans. In a large pot, cover the beans in water and soak overnight, then drain them. If you are in a hurry and don't have time to soak the beans overnight, place the beans in a bowl and pour boiling water over them. Once they have expanded and soaked up most of the water, proceed.

Place the beans in a deep pot and cover with water by 2 inches. Add the onion and epazote. Bring to a boil and then reduce to a gentle simmer, stirring occasionally, until the beans are tender, about 1½ hours, longer if the beans are old. You may need to add more hot water to the beans as it evaporates during the cooking process.

When the beans are done, discard the onion and add the salt. The beans can be made ahead of time up to this point and refrigerated for a day. To serve, reheat gently with a little water if the liquid has evaporated. Pour into a serving bowl and sprinkle with the cheese just before serving.

SERVES 8 TO 10
(Makes about 8 cups)

Rum-Banana Bake

This might not be the most authentic Mexican dish, but it goes wonderfully well with this meal and it is quick, uncomplicated, and delicious. Use a handsome earthenware baking dish so that you can bring it to the table. Assemble the dessert and put it in the oven right before you sit down to dinner.

Preheat the oven to 350°F.

Using a large flat baking dish or 2 smaller ones so that you can bake all the bananas at the same time. Slice the bananas lengthwise, and lay them neatly in the dish. Cut the butter into small pieces and scatter it over the bananas, along with the lime juice, brown sugar, and rum.

Bake for about 30 minutes. Serve with a bowl of lightly sweetened whipped cream or slightly softened vanilla ice cream.

SERVES 8

8 bananas or plantains, medium-ripe

2 tablespoons unsalted butter

Juice of 2 limes

¼ cup dark brown sugar

⅓ cup dark rum

1 half pint heavy whipping cream or 1 pint vanilla ice cream

A Greek
Seaside Soirée

Taramasalata and Smoked Salmon Toasts

· · · · ·

Greek Cheese in Olive Oil and Herbs

· · · · ·

Baked Shrimp in Garlicky Tomato Sauce with Feta

· · · · ·

Green Bean Salad with Black Olives and Arugula

· · · · ·

Greek Yogurt with Dark Honey and Roasted Walnuts

This utterly delicious and undemanding menu has its origins in Greece, where you are likely to be served these dishes at a seaside taverna. It's a good choice for a hot day.

I have been making this meal for parties for decades. The shrimp and tomato main course was one of the most requested dishes of my catering business. My partner, Flicka McGurrin, brought back a version of the recipe after spending a year in Delphi. The colorful taramasalata and smoked salmon hors d'oeuvre offers lively flavors before the mild sweetness of the shrimp, which have a natural affinity for the tomatoes they're cooked with. I love the color and crunch of the green beans and the slivered olives with the rest of the Mediterranean meal. The rich Greek yogurt dessert is sensational when drizzled with good honey—better than ice cream any day.

The beauty of the meal is in the quality of the shrimp, and while fresh shrimp are not always easy to find, serve this dish when you can.

PARTY PLAN

A COUPLE OF HOURS BEFORE

- Toast the bread
- Prepare the feta hors d'oeuvre
- Chop the onions
- Peel and devein the shrimp
- Chop the parsley
- Prepare and chill the green beans
- Toast the walnuts for the dessert

LAST MINUTE

- Bake the shrimp dish

DECORATING IDEAS

In keeping with the Greek menu, set a beautiful table with a Mediterranean blue tablecloth and crisp white napkins. Make flower arrangements of brightly colored dahlias (red, pink, orange), placing them around the room, or on the table if they are low enough and won't obscure vision.

Taramasalata and Smoked Salmon Toasts

12 slices (½-inch thick) baguette, toasted

⅓ pound smoked salmon, thinly sliced

¼ cup taramasalata

Squeeze of fresh lemon juice

Freshly ground black pepper

Handful of chopped chives

Christopher Hirsheimer, the photographer for this book, is always ready when she needs a quick stylish hors d'oeuvre, and keeps the ingredients for this treat in her refrigerator. It makes a splash fast. Taramasalata is a Greek savory spread made with salted fish roe, usually with the dried roe of gray mullet, a Mediterranean fish. It can be found in most big markets and in Middle Eastern shops.

Cut the salmon into pieces that will fit on the toasts. Put a dab of taramasalata on top of each toast, followed by a piece of salmon. Squeeze a little lemon juice and grind a little pepper over the top. Arrange on a plate and scatter the chives over all.

SERVES 6

Greek Cheese in Olive Oil and Herbs

⅓ to ½ pound feta cheese

Olive oil

Fresh or dried oregano

Place a 1 x 4-inch piece of drained feta cheese on a small plate and drizzle olive oil over the top and around the sides. Sprinkle oregano and crushed red pepper flakes over the top and serve with Pita Crisps (see page 82), or with round slices of cucumber.

SERVES 6

Baked Shrimp in Garlicky Tomato Sauce with Feta

¼ cup extra-virgin olive oil

2 medium onions, finely chopped

⅓ teaspoon crushed red pepper flakes (or 1½ teaspoons Aleppo pepper flakes) optional

1 clove garlic, minced

2 pounds large shrimp (20 to 25 count), peeled and deveined

2½ cups canned crushed, peeled tomatoes

Salt

1½ cups crumbled feta cheese

¾ cup chopped flat-leaf parsley

This is one of my favorite Greek dishes. I know, I know: the Italian rule is that one does not serve fish with cheese, but give this sprightly dish a try. This recipe is adapted from the Greek food scholar and cook Aglaia Kremezi. When I asked her about the dish she told me that Garides (shrimp) Saganaki (copper dish) was not a traditional Greek dish, but one created in the 1960s when tourists started flocking to the Greek islands—and it remains popular today. She suggests serving it as a starter, but with a crusty loaf of country bread it is plenty for a very satisfying main course. If you are unable to get good-quality fresh shrimp, seek out the best frozen shrimp.

Preheat the oven to 400°F.

In a large, heavy skillet, warm the oil over medium heat. Add the onions and sauté until they are translucent, 3 to 5 minutes. Add the pepper flakes and garlic and sauté for a few seconds. Add the shrimp and sauté until they start to turn pink and firm, about 2 minutes.

Add the tomatoes and salt to taste, and continue to cook for another 2 minutes as the sauce begins to thicken. Transfer the mixture to a large gratin dish and sprinkle the cheese on top.

Bake for about 10 minutes or until the sauce is hot and bubbly. Sprinkle with parsley before serving.

SERVES 6

Green Bean Salad with Black Olives and Arugula

This salad provides a nice crunch and good color contrast to the red-and-white shrimp dish. The beans will keep their vivid color if you wait until just before serving to toss them with the lemon juice and olive oil.

Bring a medium-size pot of salted water to a boil over high heat. Blanch the beans for 2 minutes, then taste one so you can judge the cooking time; you want them tender but slightly crisp. Cooking time should be about 3 minutes, 4 to 6 minutes for larger green beans. Drain the beans and spread them out on a kitchen towel to cool. Refrigerate or plan to serve at room temperature.

Just before serving, toss the beans with the olive oil, lemon juice, and salt and pepper to taste. Add the arugula, toss, and taste again for seasoning. Transfer the salad onto a platter. Scatter the olives over the top, along with a pinch of red pepper flakes.

SERVES 4 TO 6

1½ to 2 pounds haricots verts or green string beans, trimmed

Salt

3 tablespoons extra-virgin olive oil

1 teaspoon fresh lemon juice

Salt and freshly ground black pepper

6 ounces arugula, washed, tough stems removed

⅓ cup pitted, cured black olives, cut into slivers

Pinch of red pepper flakes, optional

Greek Yogurt with Dark Honey and Roasted Walnuts

This dessert follows through on the tasty, easy, Greek theme of the meal. There could not be a cooler, more apt dessert after the warm tomato and fish dish. I like to serve this with a bowl of fresh apricots.

Place the yogurt in a serving bowl, drizzle with the honey, and sprinkle with the nuts. Pass the yogurt to each guest.

SERVES 6

2 to 3 cups of Greek whole milk yogurt

Dark honey for drizzling

1 cup toasted whole walnuts

SPRING HAS SPRUNG

Sautéed Morel Crostini

· · · · ·

White Asparagus with Hollandaise Sauce

· · · · ·

Penne with Peas, Pancetta, and Fava Beans

· · · · ·

Bowl of Chilled Cherries

· · · · ·

Lavender and Lemon Zest Cookies

When spring comes to San Francisco, it comes quickly—there's no melting snow, just long-awaited warmth and new food at the market. I feel an urge to meet spring head-on by cooking the foods I have been longing for all winter and that define spring for me—morels, white asparagus, peas, fava beans, and cherries.

But in Paris you would hardly know that spring has arrived at some of the older, stodgier restaurants where menus remain the same all year because they must think that tourists want certain traditional offerings. But what they don't know is that most of our palates have adjusted to the seasons. We don't want a heavy cassoulet when it is warm outside. And so on a recent trip to Paris in May, I was delighted to see menus at several restaurants featuring *menu du marché*, offering the same seasonal ingredients that were being sold at my favorite open-air markets.

So when these compelling components of spring appear, I splurge and load my basket with a dinner that we eat in front of opened windows. The elfish morels get the simplest treatment possible, in a fragrant crostini. I buy the white asparagus when I see it because the season is short, and I pair it with its favorite partner, an old-fashioned hollandaise sauce. The pasta with peas, pancetta, and fava beans practically walks to the table, it is so fresh. Since the meal is filling, I end it with what to me is the ultimate spring dessert—a big bowl of plump cherries accompanied by delicate cookies.

PARTY PLAN

DAY OF THE PARTY

- Clean and sauté the morels
- Make the toast and rub it with a clove of garlic
- Peel the asparagus
- Make the hollandaise
- Cook the asparagus
- Shuck the peas and fava beans
- Blanch the fava beans
- Make the sauce for the pasta
- Arrange a large bowl of cherries

LAST MINUTE

- Cook the pasta
- Toss the vegetables with the pasta

DECORATING IDEAS

Fill a tall vase with quince or plum blossoms, they will perfume the room. Force some paperwhite narcissus bulbs in a shallow bowl filled with rocks.

Sautéed Morel Crostini

2 tablespoons extra-virgin olive oil

2 tablespoons unsalted butter

2 cloves garlic, 1 minced and
1 for rubbing toast
OR
1 stalk of green garlic finely
chopped and 1 clove garlic for
rubbing toast

3 medium shallots, minced

6 ounces fresh morels, cleaned
and quartered

½ lemon

3 tablespoons chopped flat-leaf
parsley

Salt and freshly ground
black pepper

8 thin slices of country loaf,
toasted, rubbed with a garlic clove,
and cut in half

Morels, with their spongelike pointed caps and stout hollow stems, are one of the delights of spring. They have a nutty and woodlike perfume that develops when they are cooked (morels should never be eaten raw).

Warm the olive oil and the butter in a heavy, medium-sized skillet over medium heat. Add the garlic and the shallots, and cook until translucent, a minute or two. Add the morels and swirl them around in the pan. Add a good splash of water and cook, covered, for about 5 minutes, or until the mushrooms become tender. Add more butter if necessary to keep the mixture from drying out. Squeeze the lemon over the mushrooms, stir in the parsley, and season with salt and pepper to taste. Spoon the mixture on top of the garlic toasts.

SERVES 4

White Asparagus with Hollandaise Sauce

White asparagus is more common in France than in the United States, but for those few short weeks that it is available, splurge and serve it as a special treat. It's white because it hasn't been exposed to sunlight, and has a more delicate flavor than the grassy, zesty green asparagus. Serve white asparagus as a first course at room temperature.

TO MAKE THE SAUCE

Set up a double boiler system. You will need a double boiler or a metal bowl fitted over a saucepan with a few inches of simmering water in the bottom.

In the bowl, away from the heat, whisk the egg yolks with the water until the mixture is frothy. Place the bowl over the simmering water and continue to whisk for another few minutes, until the mixture begins to thicken.

Remove the bowl from the heat and very slowly whisk in the clarified butter, a little at a time. Whisk in the lemon juice and salt and white pepper to taste. Keep the sauce warm over warm water. If the sauce becomes too thick, whisk in a few more drops of warm water.

TO PREPARE THE ASPARAGUS

Snap the ends off the asparagus. Carefully peel the stalks to the beginning of the tip.

Bring about 2 inches of water to a boil in two large, heavy skillets. Arrange the asparagus with the tips facing in one direction in the boiling water and lower the heat to medium-high. Cook the asparagus for 20 to 30 minutes, or until very tender when pierced with a fork.

Using tongs, carefully remove the asparagus from the water and drain on kitchen towels. Then arrange on a platter, with the tips all pointed in the same direction, and pour the hollandaise over the tips.

SERVES 4

(Makes 1 cup sauce)

FOR THE SAUCE

3 large egg yolks

1½ tablespoons cold water

½ cup warm clarified butter (see sidebar)

1 tablespoon fresh lemon juice

Salt and freshly ground white pepper

1 pound white asparagus

To Clarify Butter

Cut 1 stick of unsalted butter into small pieces. Place in a small, heavy saucepan over low heat. Allow the butter to melt and then continue to cook, without stirring or allowing it to sizzle, for about 15 minutes. Then strain out the heavy matter from the clear yellow liquid. Use the latter for the sauce. Allow the clarified butter to cool slightly before proceeding with the hollandaise.

PENNE WITH PEAS, PANCETTA, AND FAVA BEANS

1 pound fresh fava beans,
shelled (1 cup)

3 tablespoons extra-virgin olive oil

4 spring onions or scallions, finely
chopped, or 1 medium white onion

2 stalks green garlic, finely chopped
or 1 clove garlic, minced

12 thin slices of pancetta, chopped

12 to 16 ounces penne

1 pound fresh peas, shelled (1 cup)

12 fresh chives, finely chopped

2 to 3 tablespoons crème fraîche

Salt and freshly ground
black pepper

Parmigiano-Reggiano cheese,
for grating

Here is a nice green pasta with a little added crunch and flavor from the pancetta. Though the vegetables are cooked in olive oil, finish them off with French finesse, with a little crème fraîche. Note that for both fresh peas and fava beans 1 pound yields about 1 cup of shelled peas or beans. If you can find fine young spring onions use them, or simply use scallions or a white onion.

Bring a small pot of salted water to a boil. Add the fava beans and boil for 1 minute. Drain, then plunge the beans into ice water to stop the cooking and to keep them bright green. Drain again and slip the skin off each fava bean with your fingers.

Warm the olive oil in a large, heavy skillet over medium-high heat. Add the onions and sauté until they become translucent, about 5 minutes. Add the garlic, stirring constantly, for 1 minute. Then add the pancetta and cook until it barely begins to brown. Remove the skillet from the heat.

Meanwhile bring a large pot of salted water to a boil. Cook the pasta until al dente. Reserve a ladle of the pasta water, then drain.

Return the skillet to the heat, add the peas, and cook until they are tender, a few minutes. Add the fava beans and crème fraîche and toss gently (add reserved pasta water if mixture is dry).

Add the pasta to the skillet. Toss gently, season with salt and pepper to taste, and grate the cheese on top before serving.

SERVES 4

BOWL OF CHILLED CHERRIES

Rinse the cherries in cold water. Arrange them in a bowl, and serve with dessert plates.

2 pounds cherries

LAVENDER AND LEMON ZEST COOKIES

This recipe makes about 150 very tiny cookies. The dough is shaped into three logs; you can use all three or freeze one or two logs for a quick dessert later. For the best results, cut these cookies as thin as possible. Watch them very carefully as they bake; they can become overly brown if left a moment too long. They are well worth the attention. If you cannot find lavender petals, try 1 tablespoon of chopped thyme or settle for the lemon zest only.

In a large mixing bowl, combine the butter, sugars, egg, and vanilla and beat until light and fluffy. Sift the flour and baking soda into the mixture and mix well. Stir in the lavender petals and lemon zest.

Shape the dough into three 6- to 8-inch-long logs, just slightly bigger in circumference than a quarter. Wrap them in waxed paper or parchment and refrigerate for at least an hour.

Preheat the oven to 350°F.

Cut the logs into very thin rounds, about ¼ inch thick, and place them on ungreased baking sheets about 1 inch apart. Bake, watching very carefully, for about 10 minutes, or until golden brown. Let the cookies cool for a few minutes on the baking sheet, then remove them from the sheet to cool completely.

MAKES ABOUT 150 SMALL COOKIES

1 cup (2 sticks) unsalted butter, softened

1 cup confectioners' sugar, sifted

½ cup sugar

1 large egg, beaten

2 teaspoons vanilla

2¼ cups all-purpose flour

½ teaspoon baking soda

1 tablespoon finely chopped lavender petals

1 tablespoon finely chopped lemon zest

"Old Stove's" Waterfront Menu

Old-Fashioned North Beach Bar Drinks

· · · · ·

Parmesan–Pine Nut Crackers

· · · · ·

Pan-Fried Sand Dabs with Aioli on Watercress Salad

· · · · ·

North Beach Gratin of Chard and Salt Cod

· · · · ·

Lemon Soufflé Madeline

While I now live on Russian Hill on the cable car line, my heart is in North Beach, the next neighborhood over on San Francisco's north side. It is there that I learned how to cook from the various "old stoves"—the butchers, wholesale fish suppliers, and other Italian vendors who have put in their time at many a stove. I also picked up a lot about traditional early San Francisco cooking from the galley of the Dolphin Club, where I have swum in the chilly bay waters for over a quarter of a century.

This meal springs from my love of the simple Italian-American fare of old North Beach, and is inspired by my favorite old stove, Lou the Glue. These dishes represent the essence of the neighborhood. The heart of the meal is a combination of crisp, succulent pan-fried fish served on a watercress salad, accompanied by a gratin made with chard (that used to grow on the old-timers' roof gardens) and one of the neighborhood staples—salt cod.

We start with some buttery, crunchy cheese wafers to eat as we sip the Italian cocktails that are popular in the raucous neighborhood bars, and end with a light lemony soufflé, the perfect counterpoint to the fish that comes between.

PARTY PLAN

THE DAY BEFORE

- Soak the salt cod and rinse several times
- Make the crackers

DAY OF THE PARTY

- Assemble the gratin
- Wash the watercress and make its dressing
- Make the aioli
- Assemble the soufflé ingredients and have the egg whites at room temperature and ready

LAST MINUTE

- Cook the sand dabs
- Beat the egg whites for the soufflé and assemble it so it is ready to bake as you sit down for dinner

DECORATING IDEAS

Bring out the red-and-white tablecloths and Chianti bottles for this meal. If you don't want to go the wine-bottle-and-candle route, just have plenty of candles on the table, along with loaves of Italian bread and bread sticks (in a glass vase). Have a carafe of white wine on the table.

Old-Fashioned North Beach Bar Drinks

Ana Handleman, voted best bartender in the neighborhood, offers her recipes for the two drinks favored by old-time Italian-Americans in North Beach.

Campari and Soda
1 shot Campari poured over ice with a splash of soda, a twist of lemon, and a float of brandy on top.

Negroni
Equal parts gin, Campari, and sweet vermouth shaken with ice and poured into a chilled stem glass with a twist of lemon.

Parmesan–Pine Nut Crackers

2 cups all-purpose flour

½ teaspoon salt

Dash of cayenne pepper

1 cup (2 sticks) unsalted butter, at room temperature

1 pound Parmigiano-Reggiano cheese, grated

60 pine nuts (¼ ounce)

These wafers are light in texture but not on flavor. The recipe was inspired by Cowgirl Creamery's cheesemaker Sue Conley's recipe from her grandmother, Mary Loh. Hers are made with cheddar cheese, but these are an Italian take on the theme, using Parmesan and pine nuts.

Sift the flour and salt together in a bowl. In another bowl, sprinkle the cayenne over the butter and cream it, adding one cup of cheese at a time until well blended. Then add the flour mixture. Blend well, preferably using a mixer.

Shape the dough into 3 logs, 1½ inches in diameter. Wrap the logs in plastic wrap and chill until firm.

Preheat the oven to 400°F.

Working with one log at a time (leaving the others in the refrigerator until ready to use), cut the logs into ¼-inch-thick slices. Place on ungreased baking sheets, leaving at least ½ inch between the slices. Press a whole pine nut into the center of each slice. Bake for about 8 minutes or until light brown. Watch very carefully, as they can burn easily. Cool on wire racks.

MAKES ABOUT 5 DOZEN

PAN-FRIED SAND DABS WITH AIOLI ON WATERCRESS SALAD

Sand dabs (Citarichthys sordidus) are small flatfish that are found only around San Francisco ocean waters. When cooked quickly over high heat, the skin crisps and the flesh stays tender close to the bone. They are very easy to fillet at the table, and are best when cooked whole, bone in, because the flesh remains moist and is more flavorful. If you need a substitute for the fish, the sole family (petrale, rex sole, or flounder) is probably the closest to sand dabs in tenderness and sweetness. Or try a rouget from the Mediterranean. The fish look good on a simple salad of watercress. I like to serve aioli, a simple garlic mayonnaise, with this dish. It can be prepared in advance and refrigerated.

TO MAKE THE AIOLI

To make the aioli by hand: In a glass bowl (placed on a folded towel so it won't slide) combine the garlic, salt, mustard, pepper, and egg. Whisk until smooth. Once the mixture starts to emulsify, add the olive oil, a little at a time, in a slow, steady stream. Whisk until it thickens. Then whisk in the lemon juice, a little at a time, until all ingredients are combined. Stir in the parsley. Refrigerate until ready to use. Serve in a small bowl at the table.

To make the aioli in a food processor: Combine the garlic, salt, mustard, pepper, and egg. Pulse until blended and smooth. With the motor running, add the olive oil in a slow, thin, steady stream. Process until the mixture starts to thicken. Stop when all the oil has been added. Scrape down the sides of the bowl and add the lemon juice. Pulse until all ingredients are combined. Add the parsley, and pulse again. Cover and refrigerate until ready to use. Serve in a small bowl at the table.

TO MAKE THE SALAD

Dry the watercress and chill it in a salad bowl as you make the dressing.

In a small bowl combine the garlic, salt and pepper to taste, and lemon juice, allowing them to macerate for a few minutes. Just before serving, whisk in the olive oil and toss the watercress with the dressing.

(Continued)

FOR THE AIOLI

1 clove garlic, chopped

Pinch of salt

2 teaspoons Dijon mustard

Dash of white pepper

1 large egg

1 cup mild extra-virgin olive oil

2 tablespoons fresh lemon juice

2 tablespoons finely chopped parsley, optional

FOR THE SALAD

2 bunches watercress, washed and stemmed

1 clove garlic, minced

Salt and freshly ground black pepper

1 tablespoon fresh lemon juice

⅓ cup extra-virgin olive oil

Lemon wedges for serving

FOR THE FISH

1 cup cornmeal

Salt and freshly ground black pepper

2 large eggs

2 tablespoons extra-virgin olive oil

2 tablespoons unsalted butter

2 to 3 pounds sand dabs (about 4 to 6 ounces each figure on 2 per person)

Lemon wedges

Molto Mario and Lou the Glue Cook at My House

About eleven years ago I proposed a story about the old stoves of San Francisco's North Beach that ended up as the cover story for the second issue of *Saveur* magazine. "An old stove" is a complimentary North Beach term for someone who has put in a lifetime in front of a lot of stoves. They can be restaurant chefs, but more often they're just simply good home cooks, with many years of experience. The legendary barkeep Rose Pistola was the star of the article, and as a result, a famous restaurant (other than her former eponymous one) was named after her in North Beach.

But since Rose is now long gone, my favorite old stove is Lou the Glue, commodore of the Dolphin Club on Aquatic Park in San Francisco Bay. Lou cooks for himself and friends often at the Dolphin Club, and since that article appeared he has gotten a lot of attention. Most recently, Mario Batali came with his "Ciao America" television show to shoot Lou the Glue cooking. Much to my delight, they used my kitchen, a few blocks from the club, and made a few delicious old stove favorites, including the recipe for sand dabs that is the centerpiece of this meal.

TO PREPARE THE FISH

In a shallow dish, season the cornmeal with salt and pepper. In another shallow dish, beat the eggs with a little salt and pepper.

In two heavy, preferably cast iron, skillets, heat the olive oil and butter, over medium-high heat. Make two to three diagonal slashes on the flat sides of each fish going from left to right so that they will cook to the bone quickly.

Dip each sand dab in the egg batter, then dip it into the cornmeal mixture to coat lightly, tapping off any excess.

Place the sand dabs in the skillets, and if the butter starts to burn, lower the heat to medium. Cook the fish for 3 to 4 minutes per side, turning once. They should be brown and crisp when done.

TO SERVE

Place the salad on a large platter and carefully place the sand dabs on top. Serve with the aioli and lemon wedges on the side. (It's also nice to provide a plate for the fish skeletons.)

SERVES 4 TO 6

North Beach Gratin of Chard and Salt Cod

This flavorful gratin proved a point to me. If vegetables are deliciously well prepared, everyone, including children, will eat them. But often parents do not take the time to prepare vegetables well for children, so no wonder they turn up their noses. When Madeline and her father came to live with me, she would eat only white food. When I saw that she liked this subtle dish, rich with greens and a small amount of salt cod, I was convinced and heartened to know that I had awakened her sweet little taste buds. Even if you think you might not be fond of salt cod, give this gratin a try, it really is something to love. Always ask for skinless, boneless salt cod, and go for the thicker center cut, if possible. This dish can be made early in the day and reheated.

NOTE: You must soak the salt cod for at least 18 hours before preparing this dish.

TO PREPARE THE SALT COD

The day before, place the salt cod in a large bowl and cover with cold water. Refrigerate for 18 to 24 hours, changing the water 4 times, to remove much of the saltiness. Cover with plastic wrap or a clean kitchen towel.

Drain the salt cod, place it in a large saucepan, and add water to cover. Bring to a boil, reduce the heat to medium-low, and simmer until the cod is tender when pierced with a knife, 10 to 15 minutes. Do not overcook or it will toughen. Using a slotted spatula or slotted spoon, transfer the cod to a large bowl. Let it cool, then break it up with your fingers, being careful to remove any stray bones or pieces of skin that might linger.

TO MAKE THE GRATIN

Preheat the oven to 350°F.

Chop the chard, discarding any tough parts of the stem. Blanch it in a pot of salted boiling water for 3 minutes until it becomes tender. Drain the leaves and when cool enough, squeeze as much moisture out as possible.

(Continued)

⅓ pound skinless, boneless salt cod

2 bunches fresh chard, washed

6 large eggs

Salt and freshly ground black pepper

Pinch of freshly grated nutmeg

5 cloves garlic, minced

¼ cup chopped parsley

2 cups whole milk

¾ cup grated Parmigiano-Reggiano cheese

1 cup toasted bread crumbs (see below)

Extra-virgin olive oil

Bread Crumbs

Fresh bread crumbs are made from fresh bread, and dried bread crumbs are made from bread that is at least a day old. To make either kind: Remove the crusts from a few slices of bread. Tear the bread into pieces, and place in the food processor. Process until the bread is ground to the desired size

When measuring fresh bread crumbs, do not pack them tightly into the measuring cup or they will lose their airy texture.

In a large bowl, beat the eggs with salt and pepper to taste, the nutmeg, garlic, parsley, and milk until well mixed. Stir in the cheese and the chopped greens.

Pour the mixture into a greased 9 x 13-inch casserole. Distribute the flaked salt cod evenly over the top and sprinkle with the bread crumbs. Drizzle a little olive oil over the crumbs.

Bake for about 45 minutes, until the top is golden brown and the eggs are well set. Allow the gratin to cool a bit before serving so the flavors come together. If baked earlier in the day, reheat for about 10 minutes at 350°F.

SERVES 6

LEMON SOUFFLÉ MADELINE

I named this soufflé after Madeline, a young girl with whom I love to cook. She had never had a soufflé, so I thought it would be fun to make one with her. She got so good at it that she decided to make one for her mother for Mother's Day. We did a trial run so she could make it all on her own. I loved watching the way she separated the eggs, cupping the egg yolk between her graceful fingers, allowing the whites to separate and slip through.

This recipe works beautifully with Meyer lemons, or use blood oranges for a subtle pink hue. If you put the soufflé in the oven as you sit down to eat, it should be done about the same time you finish dinner.

3 tablespoons plus ¾ cup sugar

5 large eggs

1 teaspoon grated lemon zest

¼ cup fresh lemon juice, preferably Meyer lemon

Preheat the oven to 350°F. Place a pan of water in the oven so that it heats as the oven does. Make sure the pan is large enough to hold the soufflé dish, with the water reaching about halfway up its sides.

Butter an 8-inch soufflé dish and dust it with the 3 tablespoons of sugar.

Separate the eggs, placing the egg whites in a slightly larger bowl than the one you use for the yolks.

Whisk the egg yolks until blended. Add the ¾ cup sugar and whisk again. Add the lemon zest and lemon juice and whisk until the ingredients are blended.

Place a towel under the bowl you use to whip the egg whites so it won't slide. Beat them until they form stiff peaks. Alternatively, use a standing mixer. Fold the lemon mixture into the beaten whites, and combine so that the mixture is all yellow, but resist stirring too much.

Pour the mixture into the prepared soufflé dish and place the dish in the pan of hot water. Bake for 35 minutes, until the soufflé is puffy, firm, and golden brown. Serve at once.

SERVES 4 TO 6

An Impromptu Salmon Supper

Warm Figs Wrapped in Serrano Ham
(PAGE 98)

· · · · · ·

Grilled Salmon Smothered in Peas and Mint

· · · · ·

Corn on the Cob

· · · · ·

Heirloom Tomato Salad with Basil Vinaigrette
(PAGE 72)

· · · · ·

Blackberry-Peach Crisp

One early summer evening, as wild salmon had just come into season, I invited a few of the old friends from my catering days for dinner. We all had had our fill of salmon during that period and had avoided serving it at our own parties, but I knew that I could win them back with this splashy presentation.

The pink salmon, smothered in the flamboyant green of the peas, spring onions, and mint, is as appealing to behold as it is to taste. The hues and inherent acidity of the multicolored tomato salad play off the corn's sweetness. And again, at dessert, the play of sweet against tart in the peach and berry crisp, swathes the evening's palate of colors and tastes with a certain delicacy.

We all hung out in the kitchen, eating figs wrapped in Serrano ham, doing assigned tasks—shucking the corn, preparing the peas, and making the crisp as we caught up. By the end of the meal, everyone agreed—salmon was back.

DECORATING IDEAS

Lay branches of bay or laurel leaves down the middle of the table or arrange a lush bouquet of late spring blossoms and place it on the sideboard. If neither option is available to you, and since you will probably eventually place the platter of salmon in the center of the table, put little sprigs of fresh herbs such as rosemary at each place setting, on top of the napkin.

PARTY PLAN

THE DAY BEFORE

- Make the crisp topping

DAY OF THE PARTY

Invite friends early and ask for a little help in the kitchen. Many of these jobs are easy enough to assign to children.

- Bring a large pot of water to a boil for the corn
- Slice the tomatoes onto a platter, make the croutons, and make the vinaigrette, if using
- Shuck the peas
- Cut the green onions
- Husk the corn
- Slice the peaches into a gratin dish and scatter the berries on top
- Sprinkle on the crisp topping, and bake it as you are cooking the salmon

GRILLED SALMON SMOTHERED IN PEAS AND MINT

Four 8-ounce wild king salmon fillets (about 2 pounds), preferably with skin on, or one large slab

Salt and freshly ground black pepper

¼ cup extra-virgin olive oil

4 cloves garlic, thinly sliced

12 small spring onions (or one large white onion), thinly chopped

2 pounds English peas, shelled (about 2 cups)

½ cup dry white wine

12 mint leaves, thinly sliced

Lemon wedges

I happened to have watched Molto Mario on the Food Network the day before I was having friends over for dinner, and he inspired me. His version of this dish used a fish called porgy, but I loved the idea of the color contrast of the peas with the salmon. You could use northern halibut or just about any good boneless fish. Fresh wild salmon can be ordered on the Internet for next-day delivery if you do not live in a region where you can get it fresh. This dish is equally delicious grilled or roasted—I've provided directions for both options.

TO GRILL THE FISH

Prepare a charcoal fire, allowing the coals to produce a medium-hot fire or preheat a gas grill to medium hot.

Season the salmon with salt and pepper. Grill for 6 to 8 minutes per side. (To check for doneness, make a small incision in the fish, if it is opaque all the way through, it is done.) It should be taken off the grill a little before you think it is done as it will keep cooking for a few minutes afterwards. You do not want the salmon to be dry.

(Continued)

A Salmon Revival

For nearly twenty years I could not look a salmon in the eye. I had poached close to a thousand whole salmon over the course of my long and youthful career as a caterer. They were lovely and delicious, but I groaned silently every time a client requested salmon. When I started my second restaurant on the waterfront in San Francisco, I breathed a sigh of relief, thinking my salmon days were over. But then our customers requested salmon more than any other fish. I just couldn't shake it.

But that was before I knew David Tanis, the marvelous Chez Panisse chef who made me realize that a change was taking place in the sea of salmon, and I became born again with my first bite of salmon in twenty years.

Wild king salmon became more readily available from the Pacific Ocean—Alaska to Monterey—and a season was determined, from May 1 to September 30. Like crab, eaten in season from reliable sources—the real thing from the frigid Pacific waters is a far cry from the farmed versions. Wild salmon that contain high levels of the healthy Omega-3 oils fight for their lives—migrating from river to sea and back to the river to spawn. It is from that flight that the great taste of wild salmon is derived. Farmed salmon just doesn't cut it.

Preheat oven to 375°F.

In one or two large, heavy, ovenproof skillets, heat 2 tablespoons of the olive oil over medium-high heat. When it gets hot, add the salmon, skin side down. Cook for about 5 minutes, or until you can see that it is turning pale pink. Flip it over carefully with two spatulas (if the skin sticks to the bottom of the pan, scrape it off and discard). Add the garlic and a splash of the wine. Transfer the skillet(s) to the oven and roast the fish for 10 to 12 minutes.

Transfer the salmon to a warm platter. If the skin is still on, peel it off and discard it.

In a medium-sized skillet, warm the remaining 2 tablespoons olive oil over medium-high heat. Add the green onions, peas, and wine. Swirl the pan a few times and add the mint. Once the pea mixture is warm, a couple of minutes, pour it over the fish and serve with lemon wedges on the side.

SERVES 4

CORN ON THE COB

6 to 8 ears corn, husked

1 tablespoon sugar or a splash of whole milk

4 tablespoons (½ stick) unsalted butter

Salt and freshly ground black pepper

This method for cooking corn does away with those disintegrating sticks of butter—you roll the cooked corn around in a big pan of warm, seasoned butter. There is nothing worse than mediocre corn at the height of summer. To insure that you are getting great corn, peel back the husk and take a bite of the raw corn. If it tastes sweet, buy a bunch; if it doesn't, just buy the ear you tasted and throw it into the compost.

Bring a large pot of water to a boil. Add the sugar or milk to the water. Do not salt the water. Boil the corn for about 3 minutes.

Meanwhile, in a skillet large enough to hold all the corn, melt the butter with salt and pepper to taste. When the corn is done, remove it from the pot with tongs, tap off the water, and place it in the skillet. Shake the skillet so that the corn gets coated with the seasoned butter. Transfer to a platter and serve.

SERVES 4

BLACKBERRY-PEACH CRISP

This recipe is inspired by one from Gayle Pirie and John Clark of the fine San Francisco restaurant Foreign Cinema, where they actually show movies outdoors. The sweetness of the peaches and the inherent acidity of the berries balance the flavors that combine well with the crunch of the crisp topping. Make a double batch of topping and keep it in your freezer. Then, when you bring home summer fruit, you are just a few slices away from a very good dessert—this is good made with any member of the berry family, and with nectarines.

Preheat the oven to 375°F.

TO MAKE THE TOPPING

Place all of the topping ingredients in the bowl of a food processor and pulse until the mixture comes together with a crumbly texture. Or you can mix it in a bowl using your fingers.

TO PREPARE THE FILLING

Combine the blackberries and peaches in a bowl. Add the brown sugar, flour, and a drizzle of balsamic vinegar and toss gently. Pour into an ungreased gratin dish or earthenware dish just big enough to hold the fruit. The fruit should come up to the rim. Place the dish on a baking sheet.

Sprinkle the topping evenly over the filling. Bake the crisp until the topping becomes golden brown and the fruit is bubbling underneath, about 1 hour. Rotate the pan once.

Serve with vanilla ice cream, crème fraîche, or sweetened whipping cream.

SERVES 4

FOR THE TOPPING

1¼ cups all-purpose flour

¾ cup dark brown sugar

1 tablespoon granulated sugar

Pinch of salt

Pinch of cinnamon

½ cup chopped roasted nuts such as almonds, pecans, or walnuts

10 tablespoons (1 stick plus 2 tablespoons) unsalted butter, chilled and cut into 1-inch pieces

FOR THE FILLING

1 pint blackberries

4 to 5 peaches, peeled and sliced

3 tablespoons dark brown sugar

3 tablespoons all-purpose flour

A few drops balsamic vinegar, optional

A MIDSUMMER NIGHT'S COUNTRY SUPPER

Assorted Olives

· · · · ·

Fried Squash Blossoms
(PAGE 18)

· · · · ·

Grilled Rosemary Lamb Chops

· · · · ·

Slow-Roasted Tomatoes

· · · · ·

Cool Cucumber Salad

· · · · ·

Peach Ice Cream

Although I hate to admit it, up until last summer I had always left the job of grilling to the men, or others more confident than I. But since the meals that end up on the grill are usually my inspiration anyway, and I was buying and preparing the food, why not grill it? So I decided to tackle the grill. By the end of the summer I was no longer a novice and was grilling meat, fish, and vegetables with confidence.

This dinner is born out of my love for meat and particularly succulent lamb chops. I cooked a version of this Sunday supper for my favorite bakers, Ed and Kathleen Weber, whose delicious Della Fattoria bread has made my life in San Francisco so much better. I wanted to bring dinner to them so that they could relax at home on their only day off. I brought the ingredients to their ranch in Petaluma, and to my delight, the whole family joined in the preparation. The men wanted to grill, but I got them to go along with my self-imposed tutorial by asking them for coaching. The chops turned out perfectly—moist and aromatic with garlic and rosemary— and we all loved the way they tasted with the slow-cooked tomatoes that baked inside while we were outside enjoying the day. The cucumber salad is cool and refreshing, served with a good crusty bread, such as Della Fattoria's Meyer lemon, sea salt, and rosemary bread.

There's nothing like fresh ice cream to top off a summer meal, and with peaches so plentiful during the summer, this is an ideal make-ahead dessert.

PARTY PLANNING

THE DAY BEFORE

- Make the marinade
- Marinate the chops
- Make the ice cream

DAY OF THE PARTY

- Start the tomatoes early in the day before it gets hot outside
- Make the cucumber salad
- Make the peach ice cream

LAST MINUTE

- Start the fire 20 to 30 minutes before you want to start grilling

DECORATING IDEAS

A brilliant designer friend of mine came up with a handsome table decorating idea for a Sunday supper: painting multicolored stripes—chartreuse, red, orange, yellow, green—on long sheets of brown wrapping paper. They were amusingly haphazard. He rolled the paper right down the middle of the table and creased the ends. We used multicolored napkins to match the stripes. When the party was over, the paper went into the compost bin. When you bring a party to friends, this might be a fun thing to do because you do not have to involve them in the table-setting process, you bring everything.

GRILLED ROSEMARY LAMB CHOPS

FOR THE MARINADE

3 cloves garlic, minced

¼ teaspoon salt

¼ teaspoon freshly ground black pepper

3 tablespoons fresh rosemary leaves, chopped

2 tablespoons extra-virgin olive oil

Pinch of crushed red pepper flakes, optional

FOR THE CHOPS

12 loin or rib lamb chops

Rosemary sprigs for garnish

You can't miss with well-seasoned lamb chops. The type of chops to use is entirely up to you. I love the way the rack chops look with their long rib bones exposed, but you can use shoulder chops just as well. Figure on two chops per person.

TO MAKE THE MARINADE

In a small bowl, whisk together all the marinade ingredients. Rub the marinade on the chops, and refrigerate for at least 30 minutes or overnight.

TO PREPARE THE CHOPS

Prepare a fire and allow the coals to die down to a medium-hot temperature or preheat a gas grill to medium-high.

Cook the chops for 6 to 7 minutes per side or until firm and resilient to the touch for medium, about 5 minutes per side for rare-pink. Make a slit into one of the chops to test for doneness to your liking, but take them off the grill while still slightly pink as they will continue to cook as they rest. Transfer them to a platter and serve with a rosemary sprig on top.

SERVES 6

Slow-Roasted Tomatoes

24 to 36 medium-sized round, ripe, but not overly juicy, tomatoes (about 3 pounds)

Salt and freshly ground black pepper

Extra-virgin olive oil, to drizzle

Balsamic vinegar

1 clove garlic, minced

⅓ to ½ cup fresh chopped herbs: any combination of parsley, marjoram, oregano, chervil

¼ cup grated Parmigiano-Reggiano cheese, optional

What a tasty combination these juicy tomatoes make with the lamb. They're pretty on the plate, too. If you can get a colorful mixture of vine ripened tomatoes, it makes for a dramatic presentation. You could use red and yellow cherry tomatoes, cut in half, and some bigger yellow, red, and orange tomatoes and perhaps some green striated ones as well. It is a good idea to serve them in the dish in which they were baked because the juices are pretty tasty sopped up with a piece of bread.

Preheat the oven to 250°F.

Core the tomatoes and cut them in half width-wise. Place the halves in one or two baking dishes cut side up. Sprinkle with salt and pepper. Drizzle with olive oil and a few drops of balsamic vinegar.

Bake for 3 or 4 hours, or until the tomatoes soften and almost collapse. (Alternatively, place the tomatoes in a 350°F oven and bake for about an hour.) Fifteen minutes before the baking is completed, combine the garlic and herbs in a small bowl. Remove the tomatoes from the oven and sprinkle the herbs and cheese on top of the tomatoes.

Serve warm or at room temperature.

SERVES 6 TO 8

COOL CUCUMBER SALAD

This salad has an unexpected herby punch. If you don't like anchovies, omit them.

Using a mortar and pestle, pound the garlic and salt together to make a paste. Add the capers and anchovies and pound again. Add the vinegar and pepper and mix with a fork. Then add the olive oil and mix again with a fork and transfer to a bowl. Alternatively, you can chop the ingredients and mix them in a bowl. Allow the flavors to mingle as you cut the cucumbers.

If using short cucumbers, peel them, then cut in half lengthwise. Scoop out any seeds with a teaspoon. If using English cucumbers, neither peeling nor seeding is necessary. Cut the cucumbers on the diagonal into thin slices.

In a bowl, pour the dressing over the cucumbers and toss to coat them. Pour the mixture onto a serving platter and scatter the marjoram leaves over the top. Grate the salata ricotta or crumble the feta cheese over the top. Chill before serving.

SERVES 6

1 clove garlic

Salt

2 tablespoons capers, preferably salt-packed, soaked and rinsed

3 anchovy fillets, roughly chopped

2 tablespoons red wine vinegar

Generous pinch of freshly ground black pepper

½ cup extra-virgin olive oil

2 English cucumbers or 4 cucumbers

2 tablespoons chopped fresh marjoram leaves or oregano

2 ounces salata ricotta, or feta cheese

PEACH ICE CREAM

One of the joys of making ice cream at home is eating it the second it is done. I often prepare an ice cream mixture ahead of time and then pour it into the frozen container (that's always ready in my freezer) and turn it on just as I sit down for dinner. Then both the ice cream and dinner will be done at the same time. Alternatively, you can make the ice cream ahead of time and scoop it into a container and store it in the freezer until you are ready for dessert.

Combine the peaches and sugar in a large bowl, or in the bowl of a food processor. Mash with your hands or pulse until combined but not totally pureed.

Add the milk and cream and mix well. Pour into an ice-cream maker and freeze according to the manufacturer's instructions.

SERVES 4 TO 6

4 large, very ripe peaches, peeled and pitted

¾ cup dark brown sugar (adjust amount according to the sweetness of the peaches)

1 cup whole milk

1 cup heavy whipping cream

RUSSIAN HILL WRITERS' GROUP DINNER

Heirloom Tomato Salad with Basil Vinaigrette

· · · · ·

Seared Tuna Steaks with Tonnato Sauce

· · · · ·

Orzo with Garden Herbs

· · · · ·

Green Salad with Extraordinary
Shallot Vinaigrette
(PAGE 118)

· · · · ·

Lemon Granita

I happily agreed to make this meal for my friend Terry Gamble and her writers' group. The members generally take turns cooking, so when Terry suggested that I cook the week that it was her turn, I was delighted to have the opportunity to cook for them and hear them read their work. We ate, they read their latest work, and we all talked about food. We talked about the effect that writing about food can have on a manuscript, how it can make it juicier and more sensuous. As a result of this dinner, I was asked to be an honorary member of the group. This just goes to show the positive effect that a good dinner can have.

This is an extraordinarily easy last-minute dinner menu—a simple salad, seared fish, a quick pasta on the side—just the sauce for the tuna and the dessert need to be made ahead of time. You need only to sear the tuna, slice the tomatoes, and throw the orzo together with chopped herbs right before dinner. A good crusty baguette is just the thing to sop up all the good juices from the tuna sauce and tomato salad. Any dessert with lemon makes a cool culmination to a fish dinner, and this lemon granita is the perfect summertime choice.

PARTY PLAN

THE DAY BEFORE

- Make the tonnato sauce

DAY OF THE PARTY

- Toast the croutons
- Make the vinaigrette
- Chop the herbs for the orzo
- Grate the Parmigiano-Reggiano
- Make the granita

DECORATING IDEAS

Place a handsome wooden bowl with lots of lemons in the center of the table, with lemon leaves inserted around the edges. Place baguettes down either side of the table for easy serving—instead of slicing the bread, ask your friends to break off pieces.

Heirloom Tomato Salad with Basil Vinaigrette

FOR THE CROUTONS

½ to ¾ of a crusty country loaf

2 tablespoons extra-virgin olive oil

Salt and freshly ground
black pepper

FOR THE DRESSING

¼ teaspoon sea salt

1 large shallot, finely diced

2 tablespoons red wine vinegar

½ cup extra-virgin olive oil,
excellent quality

Freshly ground black pepper

FOR THE SALAD

4 to 5 pounds tomatoes, preferably
heirloom and multicolored, sliced

1 pint cherry tomatoes, preferably
multicolored, halved

Sea salt and freshly ground
black pepper

Handful of fresh basil leaves torn
or cut into thin strips

I cannot wait for the day in July or early August when I smell that evocative, earthy aroma of ripe heirloom tomatoes at my farmers' market. I buy them at the almost-bursting stage. At home, I toss them with basil, garlic, penne, and olive oil; I make Greek salads; I roast them for hours in the oven. Then I long for the taste of the simple arrangement of sliced tomatoes like this, with a chiffonade of basil, some crystals of sea salt, and the vinaigrette.

TO PREPARE THE CROUTONS

Preheat the oven to 200°F.

Tear the bread into small pieces about the size of a quarter. On a baking sheet toss the bread with the olive oil and salt and pepper to taste. Bake until the croutons are toasty and crunchy, about 30 minutes. Watch carefully. Turn the oven off and leave them until you are ready to toss the salad.

TO MAKE THE DRESSING

Place the sea salt in a small bowl and add the shallot and vinegar. Let the shallot macerate for 10 minutes. Just before serving, whisk in the olive oil until well blended. Add pepper to taste.

TO SERVE

Arrange the tomatoes on a large white platter, scattering the cherry tomatoes over the top. Spoon the dressing lightly over the tomatoes, season with salt and pepper, and scatter the croutons and basil on top

SERVES 4 TO 6

Chiffonade

Cutting a leaf into chiffonade provides a feathery uniform cut for herbs. Stack the leaves, one on top of the other with spines facing upward. Roll the leaves and cut off slices crosswise so you end up with thin elegant strips of the basil. Works for mint, too.

Seared Tuna Steaks with Tonnato Sauce

FOR THE SAUCE

One 6-ounce can imported tuna (packed in oil), drained

6 anchovy fillets, chopped

3 cloves garlic, minced

3 tablespoons capers (preferably salt-packed), soaked and rinsed

1 tablespoon Dijon mustard

1 tablespoon grainy mustard

3 to 4 large egg yolks

½ cup extra-virgin olive oil

3 tablespoons fresh lemon juice

Freshly ground black pepper

FOR THE TUNA

6 tuna steaks, 4 to 6 ounces each and about 2 inches thick

Salt

1 tablespoon black peppercorns

¼ cup extra-virgin olive oil

A handful of flat parsley leaves

Lemon wedges

2 tablespoons capers, soaked and rinsed

Tonnato sauce—a creamy mayonnaise brought to extraordinary heights by the addition of anchovies and tuna—is traditionally served with veal. Few people cook veal these days, but I didn't want to let this luscious sauce disappear from my repertoire. So I spoke with one of my favorite chefs, Steve Johnson, who suggested an alternative to veal. This "double tuna" dish was one of the most popular items on the menu at his former restaurant in Cambridge, Massachusetts, The Blue Room. It's a versatile dish that can be served hot or cold.

The quality of tonnato sauce depends upon the excellence of imported tuna packed in oil. Since it really is a sort of rough mayonnaise, this is one of the rare occasions that I think a food processor works best, but you can also mix the ingredients by hand.

TO MAKE THE SAUCE

In the bowl of a food processor, combine the tuna, anchovies, garlic, and capers and pulse to mix well. Add the mustards and egg yolks, and pulse to blend. With the motor running, add the olive oil in a slow, steady stream. As the sauce thickens, balance the seasonings with lemon juice, and pepper to taste. Transfer to a bowl and refrigerate.

Tips for Cooking Tuna

Tuna cooks very quickly, so a hot pan on the stove is generally a better choice than grilling the delicate fish because you can control the heat and the doneness of the fish. But if you prefer to grill, make sure you do not overdo it—cook the tuna over a medium-hot fire for about 4 to 5 minutes per side. Cut into one of the steaks to make sure it is translucent in the middle.

FOR THE STOVETOP

If the steaks are 2 inches thick, cook for 2½ to 3 minutes per side. If they are less than 2 inches thick, cook for 1½ to 2 minutes per side.

The Old-Time Butcher

When I had my first restaurant in San Francisco's North Beach, we were half a block from the best Italian butcher in town. Mr. Iaocopi was a huge, gruff man with a tender heart and an admiring eye. He knew more about meat than anyone I had ever known, and he was my mentor when it came to its preparation. He didn't trust people who were not fond of meat, and was delighted when I told him that my romance with a vegetarian had ended. We would discuss the neighborhood and our love lives, but as the years passed, he really was most interested in what I was making for dinner. I'd often stop by, as he made sausages or was preparing veal for fancy Italian restaurants in town. During the summer months I loved to watch him wrap veal in kitchen towels so they would hold together during the poaching process for that heavenly Northern Italian dish *vitello tonnato*.

Today, Mr. Iacopi and most butchers like him are long gone. I have a hard time these days finding good veal. So I hope that Mr. Iacopi would approve of the way in which I have adjusted this classic Italian dish to our twenty-first-century tables, keeping his *tonnato* sauce going—on fish instead of veal—for another generation.

TO PREPARE THE TUNA

Arrange the steaks on a platter. Crush the peppercorns with the salt in a mortar and pestle or in a small spice grinder. Press the mixture into each steak.

Heat two large, heavy skillets over medium-high heat. Add the oil, swirl it around and then add the steaks. Cook for 2 to 3 minutes until browned, turn and cook 2 to 3 minutes more, just until rare. Do not overcook. Alternatively, see the sidebar (opposite) for grilling tips.

Transfer the steaks to a serving platter.

TO SERVE

If serving hot, pour a little sauce over the top of the tuna steaks and serve the rest alongside. If serving cold, sear the tuna ahead of time and refrigerate. When you are ready to serve, pour half the sauce on a platter, slice the tuna into half-inch-thick medallions and pour the rest of the sauce over the top. You can refrigerate it until ready to serve.

Either way, scatter the capers and a few parsley leaves over the top, and serve with plenty of lemon wedges.

SERVES 6

ORZO WITH GARDEN HERBS

10 ounces orzo

2 tablespoons extra-virgin olive oil

2 tablespoons each chopped chives, oregano, thyme, flat-leaf parsley, and marjoram leaves (or available herbs)

⅓ cup grated Parmigiano-Reggiano cheese

Sea salt and freshly ground pepper

Orzo is a tiny rice-shaped Italian barley pasta. It looks like rice but tastes like pasta with its flavor and bite. Here, combined with a handful of garden herbs, it stands up well to the deep flavors of the tonnato sauce, which it will mingle with on the plate.

Bring 3 quarts of well-salted water to a boil over high heat. Add the orzo and cook for 8 to 10 minutes, stirring occasionally. Drain well.

Transfer the orzo to a serving bowl. Stir in the olive oil, herbs, and cheese. Add salt and pepper to taste. Serve warm.

SERVES 4 TO 6

LEMON GRANITA

A classic Sicilian dessert, this treat brings a tart sweetness to the end of the meal. It takes about 10 minutes to prepare and 2 to 3 hours to freeze. You will need to be around as the granita freezes, as it needs to be stirred every half an hour or so.

NOTE: If you do not have superfine sugar, place granulated sugar in the bowl of a food processor and pulse for 30 seconds to pulverize.

Place the zest, water, mint leaves, and sugar in a small heavy saucepan over medium heat. Stir until the sugar dissolves, about 1 minute. Remove from the heat and allow the syrup to cool slightly in the refrigerator. When chilled, remove the lemon zest and the mint sprigs.

Stir the lemon juice into the chilled syrup. Taste to make sure the mixture is not too tart, if it is, add a little more sugar.

Pour the mixture into a 9 x 13-inch shallow baking dish (metal, ceramic, or glass), so that the mixture is about an inch deep. Place in the freezer. Every 30 minutes, stir with a fork, scraping the crystals down from the side of the dish.

When the granita is slightly slushy but definitely frozen hard, with small firm granules of ice, it is done. It will take 2 to 3 hours. (The granita may be stored in an airtight container for a couple of hours before serving.)

Take the granita out of the freezer about 10 minutes before serving, so it softens slightly. Serve in dessert bowls or glasses.

SERVES 6

Zest of 1 lemon, grated

3 cups spring water

Two sprigs fresh mint

⅔ cup superfine sugar

1 cup fresh lemon juice

A Summer Birthday Lunch

Southern-Spiced Pecans

· · · · ·

Pita Crisps

· · · · ·

Dazzling Salad Towers

· · · · ·

Summer Meringue with Berries

Daryl, a brilliant English barrister now practicing law in San Francisco, and I had been working on a business transaction for months when, coincidentally, the deal closed on the same day as her birthday. We had become close over the course of the ordeal, and it was an ideal excuse to celebrate by making her a special lunch. It was an uncharacteristically warm summer day in San Francisco, so the centerpiece of the meal was a striking multicolored tower of four summer salads. I am not normally a fan of gastronomic towers, but I love the festive look of this salad and the taste. It was inspired by a stacked salad I had at Café Marly at the Louvre. Theirs is made with crab, but I substitute shrimp when crab is not in season.

Since this is a summer lunch, a light appetite-piquing hors d'oeuvre such as roasted nuts and an assortment of olives are ideal to nibble on while sipping a glass of champagne. The cool, four-layered salad towers are stylish and dramatic, with one delicious salad piled upon another, the lemony shrimp crowning the top. When the tower walls eventually tumble, pita crisps scoop up the salad mélange.

Everyone is always dazzled by the crunchy, vibrant meringue dessert topped with sweetened cream and a scattering of summer berries. While it is festive and rich, it is not filling. It is just about my favorite dessert to make for birthdays.

PARTY PLAN

THE DAY BEFORE

- Make the meringue
- Roast the nuts

DAY OF THE PARTY

- Make the four salads in separate bowls
- Make the pita crisps

LAST MINUTE

- About 15 minutes before lunch, assemble the salad towers
- Whip the cream for the meringue

DECORATING IDEAS

In her thank-you note, Daryl described my table as "a Provençal dream with its olive branches, lavender, and lemon." Uncharacteristically, I had not thought of a table decoration, so at the last minute, I went out of my front door on Hyde Street and cut a dozen or so olive branches off the trees. I lay them down the middle of my yellow tablecloth and added lemons and lavender stalks here and there.

Dazzling Salad Towers

FOR THE SHRIMP SALAD

1 bay leaf

6 peppercorns

½ cup white wine

Salt

1½ pounds large shrimp
(20–25 count)

2 tablespoons fresh lemon juice

Splash of extra-virgin olive oil

2 green onions, minced

FOR THE TOMATO SALAD

4 large tomatoes, cored and diced

Salt and freshly ground black pepper

1 clove garlic, minced

10 large basil leaves cut into thin strips (chiffonade)

2 tablespoons extra-virgin olive oil

FOR THE AVOCADO SALAD

Prepare a half recipe of Authentic Guacamole (page 33)

FOR THE CUCUMBER SALAD

Prepare a half recipe of Cool Cucumber Salad (page 69). Chop the cucumbers instead of slicing them.

A refreshing dish for a hot day, the "tower" is composed of four salads: shrimp, tomato, avocado, and cucumber. There are two ways to serve this meal. For the tower effect you will need a 4- or 5-inch metal ring open on the top and bottom that you can buy at a cooking or hardware store. Or you can use a clear glass cylindrical bowl, and just layer in the salads (like a trifle). The salads can be made separately in advance and assembled just before serving.

TO MAKE THE SHRIMP SALAD

Bring 1 cup of water, the bay leaf, wine, peppercorns, and salt to a boil in a small pot. Add the shrimp, reduce the heat to a moderate simmer, and cook for about 4 minutes, or until the shrimp turn pink. Drain, rinse briefly in cold water, and spread out on the side of the sink until cool.

Peel and devein the shrimp. Place the shrimp in a bowl and toss with the lemon juice, olive oil, and green onions. Cover and refrigerate. (This can be done hours before the party.)

TO MAKE THE TOMATO SALAD

Place the tomatoes in a bowl and toss with salt and pepper to taste, the garlic, basil, and olive oil. Cover and refrigerate. Right before assembling, transfer the salad to a colander to drain the excess juices.

TO ASSEMBLE THE STACKED SALAD

Place one 4-to 5-inch ring in the center of a dinner plate. Gently spoon in a layer of the avocado salad and smooth it with the back of the spoon. Using a slotted spoon, place a layer of the tomato salad on top of the avocado salad. Then using a slotted spoon, place a layer of the cucumber salad on top of the tomato salad. Arrange a layer of shrimp salad attractively on top of the cucumber salad.

Very gently remove the ring. Repeat the procedure for each serving. Some of the juices will seep out around the stack; sop them up with a paper towel just before serving.

Alternatively, You can assemble the salad in a 2-quart cylindrical glass bowl so that you can see the layers. If you don't have one, just use a wooden

salad bowl, but the joy of this dish is in seeing the gradations of color and texture. Start by spooning the avocado salad in one layer, followed by the tomato salad, then top with the cucumber salad. Arrange the shrimp salad attractively on top.

SERVES 6

Southern-Spiced Pecans

5 cups pecan halves (about 20 ounces)

2 teaspoons sea salt

Pinch of cayenne pepper

Pinch of freshly ground black pepper

1 tablespoon minced rosemary leaves

1 tablespoon dark brown sugar

3 tablespoons unsalted butter, melted

These slightly spicy, herby roasted nuts are sweet and salty at the same time. They are divine to eat before dinner and are versatile too: you can crumble them on top of pumpkin pie or add them to salads. (Adapted from a recipe in Frank Stitt's Southern Table cookbook.)

Preheat the oven to 350°F.

Scatter the pecans in one layer on one or two baking sheets. Roast for about 15 minutes or until they become aromatic. Transfer the pecans to a bowl and toss with the remaining ingredients until they are well coated. Return the nuts to the oven for 3 minutes but watch them carefully, they burn easily.

MAKES ABOUT 5 CUPS

Pita Crisps

1 package small pita breads

Extra-virgin olive oil

Salt

Whenever I serve these pita crisps, guests wonder what they are—they are so good and straightforward.

Preheat the oven to 400°F.

Cut the pitas into quarters and separate each triangle at the fold. Figure on about 3 to 4 pieces per person.

Arrange the triangles rough side up on a baking sheet and drizzle them with olive oil and sprinkle with salt. Bake, watching carefully, for about 10 minutes or until light brown. Serve in a basket lined with a linen napkin.

MAKES ABOUT 4 DOZEN

Summer Meringue with Berries

What an absolutely stunning summer dessert—light, colorful, and pleasingly crunchy. For me this serves as a festive summertime birthday cake. I make it for my own birthday party and as birthday presents all summer long for my meringue-loving friends. Its success depends upon a bit of patience—patience not to hurry the meringue.

Buy long, slender candles, as they won't crush the meringue as you stick them in. If the meringue cracks a bit, don't worry, the whipped cream and berries are the perfect cover-up.

TO MAKE THE MERINGUE

Preheat the oven to 225-250°F. Line a baking sheet with parchment paper. Using a 10- to 11-inch circle (a cake pan or a plate will do) trace a circle on the parchment with a pencil. Set aside.

(Continued)

FOR THE MERINGUE

5 large egg whites or 6 medium/small whites, at room temperature

1 cup sugar, preferably superfine

1 sheet parchment paper

FOR THE TOPPING

½ pint heavy whipping cream

2 tablespoons superfine sugar or confectioners' sugar

A handful each of blueberries, blackberries, raspberries, or other fresh berries, rinsed and dried

Make sure the bowl you use is very clean, and to be extra sure, wipe it and the mixer paddles with white vinegar (this helps in stabilizing the eggs and gets rid of any oil or fat that might be lingering). Use the freshest eggs you can find.

Place the egg whites in a large bowl and beat them on medium/high speed with an electric mixer until soft peaks form. Gradually add the sugar, a tablespoon at a time, until the meringue forms stiff, shiny peaks. Then whip at high speed for about a minute or two longer.

Using a rubber spatula, scoop the meringue mixture onto the parchment circle and spread it out to the edges, flattening the top so that the sides are even and contained within the circle.

Bake in the upper third of the oven for 1½ to 2½ hours, depending upon your oven, until the meringue is crisp and dry. To check for doneness, lift it up carefully with a spatula and tap the bottom of the meringue; if it has a hard, hollow sound and the top is crisp and well set, it is done.

Do not remove the parchment, it will keep the meringue intact until ready to serve.

TO PREPARE THE TOPPING

In a medium bowl, beat the cream and sugar together with an electric mixer until soft peaks form.

TO ASSEMBLE

The dish is best assembled just as you are about to serve it but it will hold nicely for half an hour or more. Peel the parchment off the meringue and place the meringue on a 12-inch platter. Spread the whipped cream over the cooled disk and scatter the berries over the top.

To serve, make nice clean cuts through the meringue with a sharp knife, into pie-shaped wedges.

SERVES 6 TO 8

SOMEONE-CAUGHT-A-FISH DINNER

Roasted Almonds

· · · · ·

Whole Herb-Wrapped Fish with Oreganato Sauce

· · · · ·

Green Salad

· · · · ·

Oven-Roasted Summer Vegetables

· · · · ·

Fig Clafoutis

My friend Angelo Garro is a forager, fisherman, hunter, metal artisan, and a remarkable cook. He organizes all sorts of food-related outings with his friends—olive picking, eeling expeditions, boar hunts, and fishing for sea bass. He is the center of the culinary life to his friends in San Francisco.

Sometimes when I invite Angelo for dinner he'll tell me he's caught a fish and wants to bring it for dinner. Once I hear this, I call my friends and ask them to pick herbs from their gardens so that Angelo can wrap his fish and I can make a green sauce. The vegetables will be ready to be cooked at the last minute.

This menu focuses on a stunning dish that is the centerpiece (literally and figuratively) of the meal—a whole fish wrapped in aromatic herbs and grilled as the rest of the meal is cooking inside. You don't need to have a fisherman in your life to pull off a party like this; the herb-wrapped fish works equally well with a whole fish from your fishmonger.

I like to start this delicious meal with roasted almonds. They are crunchy and light and don't fill my guests up when there is such a great meal to come. The colorful roasted vegetables make a vivid accompaniment to the fish. Be sure to have a crusty loaf of bread on hand and perhaps a crisp green salad to follow the fish course. There is something summery and Mediterranean about fish followed by figs, so a creamy fig clafoutis makes a fitting finale to this special meal.

PARTY PLAN

THE DAY BEFORE

- Gather lots and lots of herbs, lemon leaves, artichoke leaves, or bay branches
- Roast the almonds
- Soak the dried figs, if using

DAY OF THE PARTY

- Prepare the roasted vegetables
- Make the oreganato sauce
- Wrap the fish in the herbs or branches
- Make the clafoutis
- Prepare a charcoal fire big enough to cook the fish, or preheat a gas grill

DECORATING IDEAS

A beautiful oval platter on which to serve the fish in the center of the table is all the decoration the table could possibly need. If you have extra herbs or branches, place them in the center of the table and put the fish platter on top.

ROASTED ALMONDS

Shown on page 159

1 pound fresh almonds

2 teaspoons salt

1 tablespoon unsalted butter, melted

This recipe is my basic standby hors d'oeuvre. I roast a couple of pounds of nuts a week and always have them ready to serve with drinks. The perfect thing to nibble on before a big meal, they are salty and crunchy and keep the appetite at bay without filling you up. Almonds are superb with a glass of dry sherry. They can be roasted earlier in the day and reheated just before serving, or just served as is. Be sure to buy fresh, unroasted, organic almonds from a grower at a farmers' market or from a bin where there is lots of turnover.

Preheat the oven to 250°F.

Place the almonds in a colander and run a splash of cold water through them so they are barely moistened and can drain. Toss the almonds with the salt. Turn them onto a baking sheet big enough to hold the almonds in a single level layer (you may need two pans).

Bake for about 15 minutes, watching carefully. Shake the pan and turn the almonds over with a spatula. Return the pan to the oven, and when you hear the first crackle, after another 10 to 15 minutes, the almonds should be just about ready. One minute too long and they will burn. If you are not sure if they are perfectly roasted, take the pan out of the oven and grab a few almonds off the pan, allowing them to cool a bit. Taste, and, if they are done to your liking, pour the almonds into a bowl and toss with the butter. Serve warm or store in an airtight container.

SERVES 8 TO 10

Whole Herb-Wrapped Fish with Oreganato Sauce

This is one of those recipes that positively dazzles. It looks as beautiful before it's cooked as it looks and tastes afterward. And it's really easy to do—just proceed intuitively, follow the directions, and you will have superb fish.

The herbs on the outside keep the fish juicy and the herbs placed in the fish cavity will perfume the flesh of the fish. Note that this is not a dish that will work with tiny boxes of grocery store herbs. You will need a big bouquet of herb branches and several bunches of soft herbs. "This is slow food," Angelo says, "the cook needs to allow time for the herbs to express themselves."

The amount of time on the grill depends upon the size of the fish. Figure on 10 minutes per inch, measured at its thickest spot. If you find it easier, you can have the fish boned, leaving on the head and tail. Cutting and portioning will be easier, but you sacrifice the juiciness that derives from cooking the fish on the bone.

Prepare the Oreganato Sauce.
Prepare a charcoal fire or preheat a gas grill.

WRAPPING PROCEDURE

You can wrap the fish a few hours ahead of time or just before grilling. This is a fairly free-form procedure. I offer precise instructions, but basically the goal is to have the fish totally wrapped in herbs. Do it in a way that makes sense for you. If the herbs or leaves burn during the cooking process, don't worry, they are discarded before serving.

On a flat work surface, set aside 6 or more pieces of strong kitchen twine at three-inch intervals, long enough (about 3 feet long) to double wrap around the fish, securing the herbs to the fish, width-wise.

Divide the tough and tender herbs. About half will be used on each side. Place half of the tougher herbs directly on top of the sections of twine. The branches should extend to about the same length as the fish. Scatter about half of the softer herbs over the tougher herbs, so they will be closer to the fish and protect it.

Sprinkle the fish generously inside and out with salt and pepper and olive oil. Place some of the soft herbs into the cavity. Alternatively you can spoon half

(Continued)

---

1 recipe Oreganato Sauce (page 91)

One 5-pound whole striped bass or salmon, or a 5-pound side of another large fresh fish

Kitchen twine

Big bouquet of fresh herb branches, one foot or longer: lemon, rosemary, grape leaves

4 to 5 handfuls of softer herbs to go closer to the fish and in the cavity: chives, thyme, sage, marjoram, mint (or use one herb)

Salt and freshly ground black pepper

Olive oil (have a bottle handy)

2 lemons, sliced ½ inch thick

4 lemons for serving, cut into quarters

the oreganato sauce inside the cavity of the fish and serve the rest in a bowl, alongside. Place the fish on top of the herbs. Place the lemon slices on top, followed by the remaining soft herbs, then the remaining tougher herbs. Then start to wrap the fish into a bundle, both sides wrapped with herbs. If you do not have enough herbs to completely wrap the fish, use some aluminum foil on the outside of the herbs. (Don't worry, this recipe will work however you wrap the fish, just do not overcook it.) Tie the string securely around the wrapped fish so that you have a compact packet, "like a salami," explains Angelo.

Place the fish on the grill and cook over medium coals for about 10 minutes per side, (the grill should be 8 to 10 inches above the coals for those first 20 minutes of cooking so that the herbs do not burn and so that the steaming begins gently). Then lower the grill to about 6 inches above the coals and continue to cook for another 10 to 15 minutes per side (longer if the fish is bigger) or until a knife inserted into the center of the fish and touched to your lip is hot. Or if you do not trust this method, insert a thermometer at the thickest point until it reads 125°F.

Using two metal spatulas, remove the fish from the grill and let it rest for at least 10 minutes. Remove the herbs and twine from the outside. Carefully transfer the fish to a long serving platter. If the fish is whole, remove the spine. Drizzle with olive oil and cut into serving pieces. Serve with the oreganato sauce on the side.

SERVES 8 TO 10

OREGANATO SAUCE

Shown on page 89

Joe Simone, a Boston chef now living in California, suggested this robust sauce for fish. A versatile sauce, it is good slathered on halibut, shrimp, or other white fish. Or try brushing it on calamari before grilling, or when grilling littleneck clams in the shells, drizzle a touch on the clams as they open.

Combine all the ingredients in a nonreactive bowl, stir well with a fork and transfer to a serving bowl to serve with the fish.

MAKES ABOUT 2 CUPS

1 cup chopped flat-leaf parsley

¼ cup dried oregano

5 cloves garlic, minced

Grated zest of 4 lemons (using a microplane, preferably)

Generous pinch of crushed red pepper flakes, or to taste

1½ tablespoons salt

¾ to 1 cup extra-virgin olive oil

Oven-Roasted Summer Vegetables

2 yellow zucchini or summer squash, cut into ¾-inch-thick slices

2 green zucchini, cut into ¾-inch-thick slices

1 large eggplant, cubed

2 red onions, cut into 8 wedges each

1 fennel bulb, trimmed and sliced into wedges

3 bell peppers (yellow, red, or orange), seeded and cut lengthwise into ½-inch-wide strips

1 sweet potato, peeled and cut into ½-inch-thick slices

8 small potatoes, unpeeled, cut into quarters

½ to ¾ cup extra-virgin olive oil

Salt and freshly ground black pepper

2 fresh rosemary sprigs, or 1 tablespoon dried rosemary

1 head garlic, unpeeled and broken into cloves

This pretty dish can be made with whatever catches your eye at the market—if peppers are readily available, use lots of them. It is a rustic dish that can be made ahead of time and reheated in a warm oven or on top of the grill once the fish has come off. It's important to separate the vegetables onto three baking sheets so they are not crowded and have a chance to get crispy and brown. They take about an hour to caramelize and roast nicely.

Preheat the oven to 400°F.

Place all the vegetables in a large bowl. Add the olive oil and salt and pepper to taste. Using your hands, toss so that the vegetables are evenly coated. Arrange the vegetables on baking sheets in one layer. Distribute the rosemary over the vegetables.

Roast for about 1 hour, until the vegetables are tender and some are brown. Shake the pans during the roasting process so the vegetables do not stick to the bottom of the pan. Transfer to a large serving bowl or platter, and serve with a sprig of rosemary on top.

SERVES 6 TO 8

This classic French dessert falls between a flan and a custard. It is brown and puffy when it comes to the table. If you cannot find fresh figs in your area, use 8 ounces of dried figs, instead. It can also be made with cherries, plums, pears and peaches, seedless grapes, or apricots.

Preheat the oven to 400°F. Grease a 10-inch round baking dish and set it on a baking sheet.

If you are using dried figs, trim them and cut them into dime-sized pieces. Place them in a bowl with ½ cup boiling water and the port. Allow them to soften for about ½ hour, then drain and proceed with the recipe.

In a bowl, combine the sugar, lemon zest, and eggs. Add the cream and vanilla and whisk again. Add the flour and salt and whisk until the batter is well blended and light. Pour the batter into the prepared dish and distribute the figs evenly on top; don't worry if they sink.

Bake in the top half of the oven until the clafoutis is golden and puffed, 30 to 40 minutes, rotating it once. The center should be firm, the sides puffed and golden, and a knife inserted into the center should come out clean. Allow the clafoutis to cool a bit and then dust with confectioners' sugar. You can reheat it briefly in a 350°F oven if you make it in advance, or serve it at room temperature.

SERVES 8

½ cup sugar

Zest of 1 lemon, grated

3 large eggs

1 cup heavy cream

1 teaspoon vanilla extract

½ cup all-purpose flour, sifted

Pinch of salt

1 pound fresh figs, trimmed and cut into quarters
OR
8 ounces dried figs

½ cup ruby port

Confectioners' sugar for dusting

A Slow, Easy Meal
Under the Grape Arbor

Warm Figs Wrapped in Serrano Ham

· · · · ·

Grilled Herb-Rubbed Game Birds

· · · · ·

Torpedo Onions in the Coals

· · · · ·

Corn on the Cob
(PAGE 62)

· · · · ·

Green Salad with Extraordinary Shallot Vinaigrette
(PAGE 118)

· · · · ·

Rustic Plum Tart with
Vanilla Ice Cream Infused with Rose Geranium Leaves

One day last summer my extended family and I ended up with baskets bulging with summer vegetables and fruits from the farmers' market, having bought more than any of us could ever eat. Deciding to pool our wealth, we gathered at my brother Tony's house in St. Helena in the Napa Valley. We gave and took assignments and ended up with one of those amiable meals under a grape arbor that lasted for hours. The memory of that feast kept me going during a cold spell one long winter.

Succulent herb-rubbed game birds were the main course, and we chose other dishes that could utilize the "outdoor kitchen" as well. We managed to use the grill for the hors d'oeuvre, the main course, and side dishes. We started with figs wrapped in ham, which can be warmed in a skillet on the grill as the coals die down for the game birds. Sweet torpedo onions got wrapped in foil and thrown around the coals as the birds cooked. And since the season's first fresh corn is irresistible, we blanched and coated it in seasoned butter in a skillet on the grill at the last minute. In keeping with the uncomplicated mood of the meal, and because plums were at the almost-bursting stage, we decided to have a luscious plum tart for dessert. It's pure and simple, made with just a bit of sugar and the failproof tart dough recipe.

PARTY PLAN

THE DAY BEFORE

- Salt and marinate the birds

DAY OF THE PARTY

- Make the tart early in the day
- Wrap the figs in the ham
- Peel and wrap the onions in foil

LAST MINUTE

- Shuck the corn

DECORATING IDEAS

Having picked grape leaves off my brother's arbor and sunflowers from his garden, we scattered them down the middle of the table. The stems of the sunflowers were cut off so they would lie flat. Then we placed yellow zucchini and other summer squash around the leaves and sunflowers. Lots of votive candles were lit as the sun went down.

GRILLED HERB-RUBBED GAME BIRDS

6 game hens, squab, or poussins,
cut in half

1 teaspoon salt

FOR THE MARINADE

3 cloves garlic, minced

¼ teaspoon salt

¼ teaspoon freshly ground
black pepper

¼ cup chopped fresh thyme or
rosemary leaves

3 tablespoons extra-virgin olive oil

Pinch of crushed red pepper flakes,
optional

Herb sprigs, for garnish

I love the pure flavor of crisp, herby, grilled game birds. Sometimes we are lucky and find pheasants or guinea fowl at our farmers' market, but usually we are delighted with tender, juicy poussins (very young chickens) or fresh game hens. Whichever bird you choose, the procedure will be the same, though cooking time will vary a bit. In any case, they won't take long on the grill; watch them carefully. Do not rush the process, the coals must die down to medium-hot. Ask your butcher to halve the birds (or do it yourself, by cutting out the back and flattening them with the palm of your hand).

Occasionally I like to serve a mixed grill—with lamb chops alongside the game birds, as shown on the next page.

Pat the birds dry and season them generously with salt.

In a small bowl, stir together the garlic, salt, pepper, thyme, olive oil, and red pepper flakes.

Do not rinse the salt from the birds but make sure they are very dry; pat with paper towels. The secret to crispness is very dry skin. Stuff a little of the marinade under the skin of the birds and rub the rest on the outside. Cover, refrigerate, and marinate the birds for 30 minutes or overnight. Save any remaining marinade.

Prepare a charcoal fire or preheat a gas grill to medium.

When the coals are medium-hot, place the birds on the grill, skin side down. Cook for about 15 minutes, until they are brown and crisp. Turn and continue to cook for another 15 to 20 minutes, brushing with a little of the remaining marinade. To check for doneness, make an incision at the point where the thigh meets the body of the bird, if the juices run clear and there is no visible redness, take them off the grill. Smaller birds will take a little less time, about 15 minutes on the skin side and only about 10 minutes once flipped.

Transfer the birds to a warm platter and scatter a few sprigs of herbs over the top.

SERVES 6

Warm Figs Wrapped in Serrano Ham

12 fresh figs, not overly ripe, tough stem attachment removed OR 6 very large figs, cut in half

12 slices Serrano ham

6 to 8 fresh thyme sprigs

Fig or grape leaves for lining the basket, if available

Although prosciutto is classic, in this recipe I like to use delicious Spanish Serrano ham—its smooth saltiness is sublime with the warm, oozing figs. To cook the figs you can take advantage of the hot coals as you wait for them to die down for the birds or they can be cooked on top of the stove.

Roll up each fig in a slice of ham and place them in a large cast iron skillet. Place the skillet on the grill as you wait for the coals to die down for the game birds. (Or place them in a heavy skillet over medium heat on the stovetop.) Cook just long enough to warm the figs, a few minutes; turn them once. Using a spatula, transfer the figs to a platter lined with fig leaves, or just scatter the thyme leaves over the top.

SERVES 6

Torpedo Onions in the Coals

6 to 10 small onions, torpedo or red, peeled

6 to 10 pieces heavy-duty aluminum foil

Salt and freshly ground black pepper

6 to 10 small pats unsalted butter

Balsamic vinegar

I love sweet, red torpedo onions, the ones with points on each end. I grew up eating them at barbecues on the beach at Lake Tahoe. They are usually available for only a few weeks each summer. If the onions are large, allow for half an onion per person. If torpedo onions are unavailable, use small red onions.

Set each onion on a piece of foil, season with salt and pepper to taste and put a pat of butter on top. Sprinkle with a few drops of balsamic vinegar. Wrap in foil and twist the top.

Place the onion packets around the hot coals The onions will take about 15 to 20 minutes, depending upon the heat of the fire. When soft to the touch with tongs, remove the onion packets from the coals. Unwrap and serve. It is fine if they are a little charred.

SERVES 6

A tart is an ideal dessert for a party, as it can be made at least 8 hours in advance. I love to make this tart when plums are at their peak and utterly juicy. Use Santa Rosa plums or the small oval Italian prune plums. Both are a rich maroon-purple in color and meaty, so they hold their shape when baked. Make the tart dough at least an hour, or up to 24 hours, before rolling out, it needs a chance to chill.

TO MAKE THE TART SHELL

Sift the flour and salt together into a large mixing bowl. Add the butter and shortening, cutting it into the flour using a pastry blender, two knives, or your fingertips. Work the fat into the flour until the mixture resembles very coarse cornmeal.

Add the ice water, tablespoon by tablespoon, sprinkling it over the flour, then tossing the flour with your fingers to incorporate it. Press the dough together to form a ball. Then shape it into a flat disk, wrap it in plastic, and chill for at least 1 hour.

On a floured surface, roll out the dough into a 12-inch round. Roll the dough up on the rolling pin and lay it across an 11-inch tart pan, gently pressing it into the corners and cutting off any excess. If there are any tears, gently patch them. Refrigerate until ready to use.

TO MAKE THE FILLING

In a large bowl, stir together the sugar and cornstarch. Add the plums and toss to coat. The add the lemon juice and toss again.

Preheat the oven to 425°F.

Starting at the edge, arrange the plums on the dough, skin side down. Work your way in to the center, in overlapping concentric circles, so that the plums create a rose pattern, with very little of the shell visible through them. Pour any remaining juices over the plums. Place the tart on a baking sheet.

Bake in the bottom half of the oven for about 15 minutes, then reduce the temperature to 375°F. Continue to bake the tart for another 45 to 50

(Continued)

FOR THE TART SHELL

1¾ cups unbleached all-purpose flour

1 teaspoon salt

10 tablespoons (1 stick plus 2 tablespoons) cold unsalted butter, cut into small pieces

2 tablespoons vegetable shortening (such as Crisco)

4 to 5 tablespoons ice water

FOR THE FILLING

1 cup sugar

3 tablespoons cornstarch

2 to 2½ pounds plums (12 to 15 Santa Rosa or about 18 Italian prune plums) cut into quarters or eighths

1 tablespoon fresh lemon juice

FOR THE TOPPING

1 cup heavy whipping cream

3 tablespoons sugar

minutes. The crust should be golden brown (you can also remove a plum slice and check underneath to see if the dough is fully cooked). Keep your eye on it, rotating it once or twice to make up for uneven temperatures in the oven. If the crust starts to get dark, cover the tart loosely with foil.

Cool tart on a wire rack. The juices will thicken.

TO MAKE THE TOPPING

In a medium bowl, whip the cream with the sugar. Serve the topping alongside or on top of each slice of tart, or serve with the vanilla ice cream (recipe follows).

SERVES 6

Always Keep an Ice-Cream Maker in your Freezer

Krups or Donvier ice-cream makers make great ice cream. You can buy the fancier versions that do not need to be kept in the freezer, but these small ones work very well. I keep the freezer bowl, wrapped in plastic, in my freezer at all times. That way, I can make ice cream when the whim strikes.

I usually make the custard mixture ahead of time and keep it in the refrigerator until I am ready to make the ice cream. Then, when we sit down to dinner, I take the custard out of the refrigerator, pour it into the frozen bowl of the ice-cream maker and plug it in. It is done by the time we have finished dinner. If I use the Donvier (requiring that I turn the handle by hand) I make the ice cream ahead of time, freeze it in a tight plastic container, and then allow it to soften slightly at room temperature for about 10 minutes before serving. If the ice cream is ready before dinner is finished, I just scoop it out into a pretty bowl and place the bowl, covered with plastic wrap, in the freezer until dessert time.

Vanilla Ice Cream Infused with Rose Geranium Leaves

This is a great recipe to go with the plum tart and it's delicious on its own as well. If you are lucky enough to have a rose geranium plant growing in your garden, here is the perfect way to put its leaves to work; if you don't, you can use either fresh thyme leaves or lemon verbena leaves.

1 cup heavy whipping cream

2 cups whole milk

¾ cup sugar

24 rose geranium leaves
OR
6 sprigs fresh thyme
OR
1 small branch lemon verbena (about 6 inches long)

6 large egg yolks

TO MAKE THE CUSTARD

In a heavy saucepan combine the cream, milk, ½ cup of the sugar, and the geranium leaves. Cook over medium-high heat until the mixture just begins to boil, 3 to 5 minutes. Remove the saucepan from the heat, cover, and let the leaves steep in the milky mixture for about 15 minutes. Then pour the mixture through a fine mesh strainer and discard the leaves or herbs.

In a small bowl, whisk together the egg yolks and remaining ¼ cup of sugar until thick and pale. Add a few tablespoons of the warm milk mixture to the egg mixture, whisking vigorously. Once combined, add the egg mixture back into the milk mixture, whisking continuously.

Cook over medium-low heat until the rich custard coats the back of a spoon (run your finger down the bowl of the spoon—if the finger mark remains, it's done). Or, use an instant read thermometer; the custard is done at 175° to 180°F. Do not allow the mixture to boil.

Strain the custard again into a glass bowl using a fine mesh sieve. Cover and refrigerate until you are ready to make the ice cream (the custard needs to chill for 30 to 60 minutes). You may place the bowl into a larger bowl of ice to quicken the chilling time.

TO MAKE THE ICE CREAM

Pour the chilled custard into an ice-cream maker and freeze according to the manufacturer's instructions. When it is done, serve immediately or transfer to an airtight container and store in the freezer for a day or two. Remove it from the freezer about 10 minutes before serving time.

SERVES 6 TO 8
(Makes about 1 quart)

Mediterranean Market Fish Dinner

Warm Olives with Thyme

· · · · ·

Roasted Halibut with Sauce Gribiche

· · · · ·

Green Bean Salad with
Black Olives and Arugula
(PAGE 43)

· · · · ·

Bagna Cauda Potatoes

· · · · ·

Summer Pudding with Juicy Berries

One of my favorite French open-air markets occurs on Saturdays in the square in St. Tropez. My friends and I go early to buy sensationally fresh fish, vegetables, and fruit and rush them home to the fridge. While I love to swim in the warm Mediterranean waters and observe the antics on the beach—masses of deeply browned, oiled bodies in every stage of nudity—I really look forward to evenings so I can cook all of the ingredients from the morning's market. It's all so delectable that I usually splurge and forget how I will look on the beach the next day—the only person for miles in a one-piece, slightly forgiving, bathing suit.

Back in San Francisco, I make this meal during our normal chilly summer, where we use the stove all season long and grill outdoors only on rare hot evenings. But for warmer climates, this would be an ideal meal when the days are still warm, but the nights are cool.

The fish of the day—halibut—is succulent and evenly cooked by being poached in olive oil (or grilled if you prefer). The potatoes embellish the fish theme with their full-flavored anchovy sauce, and the green bean salad adds color and a cool crunch to the meal. For dessert an explosion of summer flavors permeates the berry-filled, trifle-like pudding.

PARTY PLAN

THE DAY BEFORE

- Make the sauce gribiche
- Make the summer pudding

THE DAY OF THE PARTY

- Prepare the green beans
- Clean the mushrooms
- Scrub the potatoes and get bagna cauda ingredients ready

DECORATING IDEAS

Place very small vases, Moroccan mint tea glasses, or shot glasses filled with mint or herb sprigs on the table. Or you might trim the stems of sweet peas and arrange them in the short glasses, and place them around the table or at each place setting. Use lots of candles, too.

Warm Olives with Thyme

Shown on page 103

¾ pound imported olives, such as Lucques or Niçoise

2 tablespoons extra-virgin olive oil

3 sprigs fresh thyme

Gently heating olives softens them and makes them plumper and very appealing.

Preheat the oven to 350°F.

In a baking dish, combine the olives, olive oil, and thyme. Bake just until the olives are warm, about 5 minutes. Transfer to a serving bowl, and serve with a small dish alongside for the pits.

SERVES 6

Roasted Halibut with Sauce Gribiche

FOR THE SAUCE

4 hardboiled eggs, peeled and grated

1 tablespoon Dijon mustard

Pinch of salt and freshly ground black pepper

½ cup or a little more, extra-virgin olive oil

3 tablespoons wine vinegar

1 tablespoon chopped fresh thyme

1 tablespoon chopped fresh parsley

6 small cornichons, chopped

2 tablespoons capers (preferably dry salted), soaked in water and drained

Poaching fish in olive oil keeps it incredibly moist and flavorful. It is important to remove the fish from the pan as soon as its done so that it will not soak up any extra oil. This dish could also be made with red snapper, swordfish, grouper, or salmon. If you'd like to grill the halibut instead, you can marinate it in salt, pepper, a little olive oil, and thyme first.

Delicious sauce gribiche brings the flavors together and adds crunch and zing to the fish. It is wonderful for both fish and shellfish, and is even good on toast or on crisp romaine leaves. Make it a little ahead of time so that the flavors will mingle. Be judicious with salt, as the cornichons and capers are salty.

TO MAKE THE SAUCE

In a medium bowl, combine the eggs, mustard, salt, and pepper with a fork. Add the oil then the vinegar, a little at a time. Stir in the herbs, cornichons, and capers. Taste and correct the seasoning if necessary. If the sauce is too thick, add a little hot water. Cover and refrigerate for up to 24 hours. Bring to room temperature before serving.

TO ROAST THE FISH

Preheat the oven to 400°F.

Place the halibut in a baking dish just large enough to hold it. Season with salt and pepper to taste. Pour the olive oil around the fish. Arrange the lemon slices on top of the fish and scatter the herbs over all.

Roast the fish for about 25 to 30 minutes depending upon the thickness. Plan on 8 to 10 minutes per inch of thickness, measured at the thickest spot. (If you are cooking a larger piece, and the ends are thinner than the center, cut off those pieces and continue to cook the fish until done. Keep the ends warm.) Transfer the fish to a serving platter and scatter a few herb sprigs over the top. Serve the sauce in a small bowl alongside the fish.

GRILLING OPTION
Prepare a charcoal fire or preheat a gas grill to medium-hot. Grill the fish for 8 to 10 minutes per inch of thickness. To check for doneness, make a small incision into the thickest part of the fish, it should be opaque all the way through.

SERVES 6

(Makes about 2 cups sauce)

FOR THE FISH

2 pounds halibut or other firm white fish (preferably 1 large, center-cut piece)

Salt and freshly ground black pepper

Enough olive oil to almost cover the fish, at least 1 cup

1 lemon, cut into thin slices

10 sprigs fresh marjoram, oregano, or thyme, saving a few sprigs for the top

BAGNA CAUDA POTATOES

24 small fingerlings or other potatoes such as red skinned, or Yellow Finns

FOR THE BAGNA CAUDA

3 tablespoons soft unsalted butter

3 tablespoons extra-virgin olive oil

2 cloves garlic, minced

6 anchovy fillets

Bagna cauda (literally "warm bath") is a Piedmontese dip made with anchovies, garlic, and olive oil to serve with assorted trimmed vegetables. Here it is used to coat the boiled potatoes, which are then roasted, yielding rich and savory flavors. The potatoes can be boiled and tossed with the sauce earlier in the day and roasted along with the fish.

Preheat the oven to 400°F.

Bring a large pot of salted water to a boil. Add the potatoes and cook until tender when pierced with a fork, 10 to 15 minutes. Meanwhile in a mortar or bowl of a food processor, blend or pulse the butter, olive oil, garlic, and anchovies.

Drain the potatoes and toss with the butter mixture in a bowl. Transfer to a roasting pan and roast for 10 minutes. Shake the pan a few times during the roasting period.

SERVES 6

(Makes about ½ cup bagna cauda)

Summer Pudding with Juicy Berries

When berries are plump, sweet, and ripe, the time is right to make this simple but dramatic pudding. No cooking is involved and it is almost like building a sand castle; this is a great dessert to make with children. The pudding must be made a day ahead of time or at least 12 hours before serving. Use a non-crusty bread that is dense and buttery, such as brioche–type bread, or thin-sliced white bread such as Pepperidge Farm—do not use a fluffy white loaf. The amount of sugar you will need depends upon the sweetness of the berries, but keep in mind the bread soaks up the juices of the berries and mellows out the sweetness of the fruit. So even if you use 3 cups of sugar, it won't be too sweet.

Trim the crusts off the bread and slice the loaf in half lengthwise.

Wash and hull the strawberries. Puree them in a food processor with the lemon juice and sugar. Place the puree in a large bowl with the rest of the berries and mash them together with your hands. You want the mixture to be somewhat chunky; some of the blueberries can be left whole for good texture.

Line a 2-quart bowl with plastic wrap so that the wrap extends over the edges of the bowl by about 4 inches. Working with your fingers, immerse a piece of the bread in the berry mixture so that it gets saturated with the juice and picks up bits of berries. Lay the bread across the bottom of the bowl. Continue the process, lining the whole bowl with saturated pieces of bread, being careful that the slices on the outside are whole and uniform. Then fill in the inside (it doesn't matter if those pieces break up) until the whole bowl is filled, pressing down in between slices. Wrap the top up very well with the extended overlapping pieces of plastic.

Put a plate on top of the plastic wrap and weigh that down with a heavy weight—a can of tomato sauce or a brick works well. Put the bowl on a baking sheet to catch any juices, and then refrigerate for 12 to 24 hours.

Whip the cream and sugar together to form soft peaks. Just before serving unfold the plastic. Invert the pudding onto a platter slightly larger than the top of the bowl, and remove the plastic. Cut into pie-shaped wedges and serve with whipped cream (or with the Vanilla Ice Cream on page 101).

SERVES 6 TO 10

2 loaves good-quality sliced white bread (about 36 slices)

3 pints strawberries

1 tablespoon fresh lemon juice

2 to 3 cups sugar

3 pints raspberries

3 pints blueberries

3 pints blackberries

1 cup heavy whipping cream

3 tablespoons confectioners' sugar

A Festive Autumn Meal

End-of-Season Gazpacho

· · · · ·

Poulet au Vinaigre

· · · · ·

Easiest, Creamiest Mashed Potatoes

· · · · ·

Red and Green Salad

(PAGE 27)

· · · · ·

Lemon Granita

(PAGE 77)

This menu of sophisticated flavors marks a transition from summer to fall, a time when the end-of season tomatoes let us tenuously hang on to summer. But at the same time, as it grows chillier, we greet the fall with a piquant chicken dish that can easily be prepared in advance.

The light, cool gazpacho, almost a salad in a bowl, is an apt counterpoint to the rich, brown, deeply flavored chicken with its creamy vinegar sauce. I have grown to love this slightly sweet and acidic dish when in France, and make it often for parties wherever I am. The pure and simple mashed potatoes are a natural foil for the chicken's flavorful juices. And for an ideal ending to a somewhat rich meal, the lemon granita plays a refreshing, citrusy note.

Decorating Ideas

Big, handsome pumpkins and Hubbard squash come to market in early fall. I buy a 15-to-20 pound pumpkin and leave it on my table, surrounded by candles, for weeks on end, always ready for a party.

Party Plan

DAY OF THE PARTY

- Make the gazpacho early so the flavors can mingle

- Make the chicken early and reheat, or make at the last minute

- Make the granita a few hours before the party

LAST MINUTE

- Make the mashed potatoes

End-of-Season Gazpacho

FOR THE CROUTONS

½ loaf rustic country bread

Extra-virgin olive oil

2 cloves garlic, crushed

FOR THE ROASTED TOMATOES
(to be made into juice)

18 to 24 ripe tomatoes

Drizzle of extra-virgin olive oil

Salt and freshly ground
black pepper

FOR THE SOUP

3 pounds ripe heirloom tomatoes, cored and diced (use some colorful cherry tomatoes, too)

1 each yellow, red, and orange bell pepper, cored and diced

1 small red onion, minced

2 cloves garlic, minced

3 to 4 tablespoons Spanish sherry vinegar

1 English cucumber, diced

2 tablespoons extra-virgin olive oil, more to top

Salt and freshly ground
black pepper

I often buy tomatoes by the case at my farmers' market, and occasionally a friend will give me an armload of late-season tomatoes. I slow-roast some of them, then pass them through a food mill or strainer. The result is a deliciously dense sauce that creates a rich base for the gazpacho.

The soup can be thinned with a little water, but I prefer a chunky gazpacho with a drizzle of olive oil and a few garlicky croutons on top. On a very hot day, float an ice cube in each bowl of soup, to keep it cold. Make it the morning of your party so the flavors have a chance to mingle.

Preheat the oven to 250°F.

Cut six 1-inch-thick slices of country bread into ½-inch cubes. Toss in a bowl with a little olive oil, garlic, and salt and pepper to taste. Place on a baking sheet and bake in the same oven that the tomatoes bake in but only for about 10 minutes, or until brown and crispy. Set aside.

Cut the tomatoes for roasting in half widthwise. Place them on a baking sheet, sprinkle with salt and pepper and drizzle with olive oil. Cook for 1 hour as long as 3 hours. You do not need to be precise about the roasting time. When they have collapsed and are well roasted, pass them through a food mill, leaving the seeds and skins behind. This process adds a deep rich flavor to the soup. The tomatoes can be roasted a day ahead of time and put through the mill to make the juicy base of the soup.

In a non-aluminum bowl, mix the roasted tomato juices with all the soup ingredients, adding enough water to create a soupy consistency. Chill for 3 hours or more. Taste for salt and pepper. Serve with a little olive oil and some croutons on top.

MAKES 8 CUPS

EASIEST, CREAMIEST MASHED POTATOES

Mashed potatoes must have been invented to go with the Poulet au Vinaigre sauce (page 112)—they pick up the strong juices and soften them. Marion Cunningham, America's great home cook, says that the trick to creamy mashed potatoes is to heat the milk (or cream) and butter together before you add them to the potatoes.

When I first started going to open-air markets in Paris and was faced with up to twelve varieties of potatoes, the names were strange and I had no idea what to buy. When I asked one of the vendors for advice, I found that the French tend to be extremely specific about which potato to use for a certain dish. For this dish, you cannot go wrong with good old-fashioned russets.

Place the potatoes in a large pot and cover with salted cold water. Bring to a boil. Reduce the heat to medium-high, and cook for 15 to 20 minutes, until the potatoes are tender when pierced with a fork. Drain.

Meanwhile in a small pot, warm the butter and milk over medium-low heat.

Place the potatoes in a large bowl and mash them with a potato masher, adding a little of the warm milk-and-butter mixture as you go. Continue to mash until the lumps are gone. Add just enough of the milk mixture to get a creamy consistency. Then whip the potatoes with a fork and season with salt and pepper to taste.

You can make the potatoes a little ahead of time and keep them warm in a low oven, well covered, until ready to serve.

SERVES 6

---

6 medium-sized russet potatoes, peeled and quartered

3 to 4 tablespoons unsalted butter

1 cup whole milk or cream (or half-and-half)

Salt and freshly ground white pepper

Poulet au Vinaigre

12 chicken thighs (about 3 to 4 pounds), bone in

Salt and freshly ground black pepper

4 tablespoons unsalted butter

2 tablespoons olive oil

6 shallots, minced

6 cloves garlic, minced

½ cup apple cider vinegar

1½ cups dry white wine

1 tablespoon tomato paste

1½ cups chicken stock, preferably homemade

½ cup chopped Italian parsley

After trying this deeply flavored chicken at several restaurants in Paris, I came home to make it again and again. Poulet au vinaigre is now one of my favorite party meals. The chicken literally takes just an hour to make from start to finish (most of the time is in the oven); or you can make it ahead of time and reheat just before serving. With a little time resting in its juices, the chicken gets even more succulent and flavorful. Just reheat it gently.

NOTE: If you are making this dish for a large crowd, remove the skin from some of the thighs, as they could provide too much fat. Be sure to pour off the chicken fat as you go.

Season the chicken generously with salt and pepper to taste. In a large, deep skillet (big enough to hold all chicken fairly close together; or use two skillets) melt 3 tablespoons of the butter in 1 tablespoon of the olive oil over medium-high heat. Brown the chicken for about 8 minutes, turning so both sides get nicely browned. Transfer the chicken to a deep, broad, ovenproof casserole that can go from the oven to the table. Remove the skillet from the heat and pour off most of the fat.

Preheat the oven to 375°F.

Place the skillet back over medium heat and add the remaining 1 tablespoon butter and 1 tablespoon olive oil. Add the shallots and garlic and cook for about 1 minute, or until they become translucent. Add the vinegar and wine, and stir up the crispy bits that have stuck to the bottom of the pan. Allow the liquids to cook down a bit, stirring occasionally, for about 8 minutes. Whisk in the tomato paste and let the sauce simmer and condense, about 5 minutes more. Then add the chicken stock, a little at a time. Keep stirring to mix well.

Pour the sauce over the chicken. Bake for 35 to 45 minutes until the chicken is very tender, turning the chicken pieces midway through, so that both sides are infused with the sauce. Remove one thigh and cut into it to make sure it is done and no red juices flow from the cut.

Remove the casserole from the oven, sprinkle the parsley on top, and serve.

SERVES 6 TO 8

CRACKED CRAB SUNDAY LUNCH— A SAN FRANCISCO TRADITION

Belgian Endive Soup

. . . . .

Fresh Marinated Cracked Crab

. . . . .

Green Salad with Extraordinary Shallot Vinaigrette

. . . . .

Cheese Course

. . . . .

Blood Orange Sorbet

San Franciscans have a serious relationship with Dungeness crab. It's our culinary anthem, the cracking of the shells is its refrain, its tempo accumulates momentum as a fortune of plump, pinkish-white meat mounds on the plate. The local delicacy, it's our lobster, our crayfish, our *loup de mer*, our *baccalà*—it's our celebration food, the food we serve when intimidatingly good cooks come to town. It's the ultimate San Francisco meal.

A Sunday lunch is a great way to invigorate a long city weekend especially in the colder months when monotonous weather has set in. And in San Francisco, the opening of crab season in mid-November is as good a reason as any to celebrate. When Dungeness is in season, I like to invite friends over, light a fire, and serve a huge platter of marinated crab. Add a hearty fall soup, a green salad, assorted cheeses, some crusty sourdough, and a refreshing sorbet, and you are all set.

The platter of crab can be on the table, and as people sit down, serve a deep bowl of satisfying Belgian endive soup. The crab is rich, subtle, and slightly briny, and this marinade brings out every bit of underlying flavor. The crab cries out for a simple salad with a perfectly balanced vinaigrette. The bread sops up the juices of the marinade and the salad and goes well with the cheese. I cannot dream of a more delicious dessert than the wildly colored blood orange sorbet.

PARTY PLAN

THE DAY BEFORE

- Make the soup
- Cook and crack crabs (or buy them already cooked)
- Marinate the crab
- Juice the oranges and make the sorbet

DAY OF THE PARTY

- Make the salad
- Allow cheese to come to room temperature

DECORATING IDEAS

It is an old San Francisco tradition to line a table with newspaper and serve cracked crab on it, tossing the shells right on the paper. But I usually spread out a tablecloth and leave room in the center of the table for the large platter of crab. Place empty bowls as shell receptacles around the table. The salad can go on the table along with the sourdough bread and the cheese. All the flavors taste good on the same plate. There is so much going on on the table that there is really not room for any additional decoration.

Fresh Marinated Cracked Crab

3 Dungeness crabs, cooked
and cracked (see sidebar)

FOR THE MARINADE

6 cloves garlic, minced

1 tablespoon salt

1 tablespoon freshly ground
black pepper

1 bunch Italian parsley, washed,
leaves roughly chopped

Sprinkling of crushed red pepper
flakes

⅓ cup fresh lemon juice, strained

1 cup extra-virgin olive oil

I used to think, as many San Francisco natives do, that the only way to serve crab was steamed or boiled. But once my friend Angelo Garro, forager and fisherman, made his Sicilian interpretation of cracked crab for our annual Christmas Eve Seven Fishes dinner, I became a convert. The crab is still in the shell, and guests must still do the work, but with an added attraction—the crab has been marinated, and as you prod the meat out, the marinade mingles with the crabmeat on the fingers for a sweet, briny crabbiness mixed with the spice of the marinade. No need for mayonnaise or lemons, all the seasonings are on the shell. It is best to marinate the crab for couple of hours before serving. If your guests are big eaters, plan on one crab serving two people, otherwise a crab will serve three. No matter what, you will have no crab left at the end of the meal.

Stir all of the marinade ingredients together and toss with the cracked crab. Refrigerate for several hours. Transfer to a large platter and place in the middle of the table. Serve with warm sourdough bread.

Place empty bowls on the table for the shells. And, unless you want your guests to get up from the table to wash their hands, as I always do, serve hot towels or finger bowls with a lemon slice floating in the water.

SERVES 6

Cooking Live Crabs

The best way to insure that your crabs are absolutely fresh is to buy them live, then cook and crack them yourself. It is not difficult and is really quite satisfying. When crabs are refrigerated they become docile. Be careful, though and handle the crabs with tongs, from the rear, so the pincers cannot grab you.

Bring a very large pot of salted water to a boil. Carefully drop the crabs in, one by one, but don't cook more than three at a time. When the water returns to a boil, cook the crabs until they turn bright orange and pink, 10 to 12 minutes. Remove them with tongs and drain them in the sink.

When they are cool enough to handle, pull off the back shell. Rinse out and discard any gills and yellow matter. Cut the crab in half lengthwise with a cleaver. Pull off the claws and legs. Lay the pieces on a towel and whack each piece and all of its sections with a mallet or a hammer to crack it.

This can be done a day ahead of time but the crabs must then be immediately refrigerated.

BELGIAN ENDIVE SOUP

This warming and welcoming soup saves any cold day. Dijon chef, Alex Miles, first served it to me on a rainy day, and it has been one of my favorite fall soups ever since. Although the soup is sumptuous served immediately after preparation, it takes on even deeper flavor if made in advance. Pimenton is a Spanish version of sweet paprika. It adds a luscious undertone of flavor to the soup (see Sources, page 217).

In a deep, heavy skillet, warm the olive oil over medium-high heat. Add the endive rounds and cook for about 10 minutes until they start to brown. Lower the heat, add the sugar, salt, and pepper to taste, and simmer for 15 minutes more, stirring occasionally.

Transfer the endive to a food processor and pulse it to a choppy puree. Return the endive to the skillet, add the chicken broth, and cook over low heat. Taste for seasoning. Add a little more sugar if it is still quite bitter and add a little more salt and pepper to taste. Stir in the cream at the last minute.

Meanwhile, heat the butter in a medium skillet over medium-low heat. Add the reserved endive strips and cook until they are soft and start to caramelize, about 8 minutes.

Ladle the soup into warm bowls. Add a pinch of pimenton to each serving and float some caramelized endive on top.

MAKES 6 CUPS

3 tablespoons extra-virgin olive oil

2½ pounds Belgian endive, 2 pounds trimmed and sliced into ½ inch rounds, the rest cut into lengthwise strips (⅛ inch wide) for garnish

1 tablespoon sugar

¼ teaspoon salt

Freshly ground black pepper

3½ cups chicken broth, preferably homemade

2 tablespoons heavy cream

2 tablespoons unsalted butter

A few pinches Spanish pimenton

Green Salad with Extraordinary Shallot Vinaigrette

1 large shallot, minced

½ teaspoon salt

2 tablespoons good-quality red wine vinegar or a combination of vinegars such as balsamic and sherry vinegar

⅓ to ½ cup extra-virgin olive oil

6 to 8 cups organic salad greens, such as red oak leaf, washed, dried, and chilled

Salt and freshly ground black pepper

A light salad is the perfect counterpoint to this meal, served after the crab to cleanse the palate. Use tender organic greens and a simple vinaigrette.

Place the shallot and salt in the bottom of a large salad bowl. Pour the vinegar over the shallot and allow the ingredients to macerate for a half hour or so. Just before serving, add the olive oil, mix well and toss with the greens. Season with salt and pepper to taste, and serve at once.

SERVES 6

Cheese Course

This menu presents a perfect opportunity to serve a platter of cheeses with the salad, or following it. The rest of the meal has not been terribly filling—satisfying, yes, but there is still room for cheese. Select an assortment, such as a goat's milk, sheep's milk and cow's milk cheese—some ripe and runny, others hard or fresh. Or you can serve just one perfect cheese; one of my favorites is Cowgirl Creamery's Red Hawk, an award-winning triple-crème washed-rind cheese from Point Reyes, California.

In Paris when I go to the cheese store, the vendor usually asks when I will be serving the cheese, then chooses the one that will be perfectly ripe for that day. If you go to a good cheese store in the United States, the purveyor should be able to help you decide on the right cheeses. There are good mail order sources, as well (see Sources, page 217).

Serve cheeses on a wooden board. Place small cheese knives by the cheeses—dull blades for the softer cheeses and a small sharp knife for the harder cheeses. Serve sliced bread such as a dark walnut crusty loaf alongside.

Blood Orange Sorbet

This is a splashy dessert that is ideal served after a fish meal. It is inspired from a Bay Wolf Restaurant recipe. The color is deep crimson and the flavor is refreshing. For a variation, you could use tangerine juice, instead.

Mix the juice and sugar together in a bowl and pour into an ice-cream maker. Proceed according to manufacturer's instructions.

Make the sorbet a few hours ahead of time. Transfer it to a bowl and place it in the freezer until about 10 minutes before serving. Remove from the freezer so the sorbet softens a bit before you scoop it into dessert dishes and serve.

MAKES ABOUT 1 QUART

Juice of 8 blood oranges
(about 1 pound)

1 cup sugar

A RANCH-STYLE DINNER WITH A FRENCH TWIST

Basket of Crisp Vegetables with Aioli

· · · · ·

Steak au Poivre

· · · · ·

Braised Fennel and Garlic

· · · · ·

Classic Spinach Salad
(PAGE 201)

· · · · ·

Double-Ginger Gingerbread

Every year I go to a cattle ranch in New Mexico to meet up with a group of friends. While they do jigsaw puzzles and ride horses, I retreat to the 1940s cowboy kitchen and cook. I am perfectly content to spend time looking out the window as I peel and chop, taking in the billowy Southwestern clouds and the sky going pink, as it can do only in this part of the country. Considering the surroundings, it feels appropriate to cook beef, but we all have had our fill of grilled steaks. I leaf through the beef recipes in the twenty-year-old cookbooks on top of the refrigerator— Ravinia Music Festival and various Junior League books. A recipe for steak au poivre jumps out at me. What a marvelous forgotten dish, so popular in the '60s. I make my own version and cannot remember a more enthusiastic response over a piece of meat and its boozy, peppery sauce.

I start the meal with a raw vegetable basket for guests to nibble on before dinner. The steak au poivre is hearty, easy, and quite delicious. Tender braised fennel makes a smooth accompaniment, providing good flavor and color, and we all know that steak and salad are great companions. The gingerbread is a dark, moist, spicy cake that is substantial enough to follow a steak without being heavy at all.

Basket of Crisp Vegetables with Aioli

4 heads curly lettuce, romaine, or mustard greens, washed

1 bunch carrots, peeled and cut into sticks

1 bunch celery hearts, cut into sticks

1 bunch radishes, trimmed

1 bunch scallions, trimmed

1 fennel bulb, trimmed and cut into ½-inch wedges

2 cups cauliflower florets, steamed

1 pound asparagus, trimmed, peeled, and steamed

2 baskets cherry tomatoes

1 recipe Aioli (page 53)

This handsome basket of crudités was our signature dish as young caterers in San Francisco. We'd vary the choices with the season, going for color and crunch. In those days we'd hollow out purple cabbages and pile in creamy leek dip. This is more of a suggestion than a recipe, since the volume depends upon the number of people you are serving.

Prepare a medium-sized basket by lining the edges with the lettuce leaves. If the basket is deep, you may need to put paper towels in the base and build up the lettuce leaves from there as you want the vegetables to fit in tightly and to look abundant. They should start about halfway to three quarters of the way up the basket.

Place an empty bowl for the aioli in the center of the basket, then build a bouquet with the vegetables, placing each type together in tight bunches. Fill in the final gap with the cherry tomatoes.

Fill the bowl with the aioli. Spray the vegetables with fresh water and place on top of a folded kitchen towel so water from the vegetables won't leak out.

SERVES 6 TO 8

STEAK AU POIVRE

Seek out the best-quality beef available for this dish. You'll get excellent results with aged, boneless strip steaks. I like to sear them over high heat so that they get a crisp, brown crust.

Lay the steaks on a flat surface. Combine the salt and the peppercorns in a mortar and pound until the peppercorns are somewhat broken up, but leave some whole. Or place the peppercorns on a cutting board under a kitchen towel and pound with a hammer, rolling pin, or the bottom of the brandy bottle, to break them up. Rub the mixture on both sides of the meat. Allow the meat to sit for at least 30 minutes, or it can be refrigerated for up to 24 hours.

Heat one large (or two medium) heavy skillet, preferably cast iron, over high heat until very hot (when a few drops of water dance on the surface of the pan, it's ready). Sear the steaks for 6 to 8 minutes on each side for rare (less if the steak is not quite 2 inches thick). To test for doneness, remove one steak from the pan after 6 minutes on the second side and make an incision. If the steaks are done to your liking, remove them; if not, cook them a minute or two longer. Remember that once off the heat, they will continue to cook for a few minutes. Transfer the steaks to a warm platter and set aside.

Pour off most of the fat from the skillet and reduce the heat to medium. Add the shallots, and stir until they are translucent, scraping up the crispy bits in the pan. Then carefully pour in the brandy. Be aware that it may flame up. Allow the flames to die and cook until the brandy is reduced by half, about 2 minutes. Pour in the cream and continue to stir until the ingredients combine and the cream reduces, again by half, 3 to 4 minutes.

To serve, you can arrange the steaks on the platter, or, cut the meat on the bias and arrange the slices on the platter. Pour the sauce over the steak and sprinkle with the parsley.

SERVES 6

4 boneless strip steaks, 12 to 14 ounces each, 2 inches thick

1½ tablespoons salt

¼ cup peppercorns

4 to 6 large shallots, chopped

⅓ cup brandy or cognac

⅓ cup heavy cream

¼ cup chopped flat-leaf parsley

BRAISED FENNEL AND GARLIC

4 pounds fennel bulbs, leafy
greens removed (with some
reserved for topping)

3 tablespoons extra-virgin olive oil

4 cloves garlic

½ cup dry white wine

Salt and freshly ground
black pepper

Here is a wonderfully successful way to braise fennel so that it is as tender as it is delicious. This dish can easily be made ahead of time and held on the stovetop for reheating.

Trim the fennel bulbs, discarding any brown exterior leaves and tough stems. Cut the bulbs in half lengthwise, then cut the halves into quarters.

Heat the olive oil in a large, heavy skillet (or two medium skillets) over medium heat. Add the fennel and cook until it starts to brown, about 7 minutes, shaking the pan so it doesn't stick and burn. Turn the fennel so it browns and caramelizes on all sides.

Add the garlic cloves and cook for 1 minute. Add the wine, season generously with salt and pepper, and lower the heat to medium-low. Cover and continue to cook for a half hour or longer, until the fennel is tender when pierced with a fork. If the liquid starts to evaporate, add a little more wine or water.

Turn the mixture onto a serving platter and scatter a few of the wispy fennel greens over the top.

SERVES 6

DOUBLE-GINGER GINGERBREAD

This moist, deeply spiced dessert is filled with a reassuring old-fashioned richness. The molasses and coffee add special depth to the flavor, and the whipped cream on top sparkles with bits of crystallized ginger. Make sure to get fresh spices—it does makes a difference.

Preheat the oven to 350°F. Butter an 8-inch square glass or metal baking dish.

In a large bowl, combine the ground ginger, allspice, cinnamon, baking soda, salt, and flour and stir well. In another smaller bowl, combine ¼ cup of the crystallized ginger, the melted butter, molasses, and brown sugar and whisk well. Add the egg and lemon zest, whisk again. Gradually whisk in the dry ingredients, then the hot coffee. Pour the batter into the prepared baking dish.

Bake for about 30 minutes or until a wooden skewer inserted into the center comes out clean. Cool the cake on a wire rack. Once cool, dust the top with confectioners' sugar. Cut into squares. (The gingerbread can be made a day in advance. Cool completely, wrap in plastic wrap, and store at room temperature.)

In a medium bowl, whip the cream and the granulated sugar together. Put a spoonful of the sweetened cream on top of each square and sprinkle a few pinches of the remaining crystallized ginger on top.

SERVES 6 TO 8

2 teaspoons ground ginger

½ teaspoon allspice

1 teaspoon ground cinnamon

1 teaspoon baking soda

¼ teaspoon salt

1¼ cups all-purpose flour

½ cup chopped crystallized ginger

½ cup (1 stick) unsalted butter, melted

½ cup molasses

½ cup dark brown sugar

1 large egg

2 teaspoons grated lemon zest (from 2 lemons)

½ cup very hot strong black coffee

Confectioners' sugar, for dusting

1 cup heavy whipping cream

2 tablespoons granulated sugar

FORAGERS' FEAST

Poached Leeks with Mustard Vinaigrette

. . . . .

Wild Mushroom Risotto with Truffles

. . . . .

Frisée Salad with Lardons

. . . . .

Pears Poached in Red Wine with Spices

One cold November night I returned to Paris after spending a week cooking in Umbria with friends. I felt a little sad, filled as I was with happy memories, having shared such remarkable times in the kitchen and at the table. But the sadness did not last for long. I had brought some Italian treasures with me: a stash of truffles that I had bought from a forager, dried porcini, and some *olio nuovo*—new peppery oil from a visit to Tuscany. I called a couple of friends on the way home from the airport and before long, we were all sitting around my table enjoying a meal in Paris, very much like what I had learned to cook in Italy.

The meal starts with poached leeks in a mustard vinaigrette with chopped egg and anchovies. It should be prepared in advance, since the woodsy, wild mushroom risotto requires last-minute attention. While it seems almost like having two salads, the traditional French bistro frisée salad with crunchy bacon (*lardons*) adds a little substance to a meal without fish, fowl, or meat, and it cleanses the palate for the dessert. And what a still life of a dessert the poached pears are, inebriated with red wine, and so fitting for the season. This meal might be a good choice for vegetarians, just omit the bacon from the salad.

Sometimes it takes a bit of foraging to pull together a spontaneous dinner, but I realized that it is easy to accomplish with a few special seasonal ingredients that can be supplemented by a trip to the grocery store.

PARTY PLAN

DAY OF THE PARTY

- Poach and marinate the leeks
- Assemble and prepare ingredients for the salad
- Poach the pears

LAST MINUTE

- Make the risotto

DECORATING IDEAS

I have a natural colored, rustic French rough linen tablecloth that is perfect for a dinner such as this. I like to pick up a few bright autumn leaves and scatter them down the table with chestnuts, walnuts, and filberts strewn here and there among them.

Poached Leeks with Mustard Vinaigrette

12 leeks, about 1½ inches in diameter, trimmed to leave about 2 inches of the green part

FOR THE VINAIGRETTE

3 tablespoons red wine vinegar

Salt and freshly ground black pepper

1 tablespoon imported French mustard, such as Dijon

½ cup extra-virgin olive oil

FOR THE GARNISH

2 hard-boiled eggs, peeled and grated, optional

2 tablespoons chopped flat-leaf parsley

2 anchovies, slivered, optional

These delicately flavored leeks make a light first course and are as good at room temperature as chilled. You might serve them on individual plates, to greet each guest as he or she comes to the table.

Cut the leeks in half lengthwise and place under cold running water to clean out any grit from the folds.

In a large, shallow skillet bring enough salted water to cover the leeks to a boil. Add the leeks, cut side down, and reduce the heat to medium-low. Cover, and poach the leeks for 5 to 7 minutes, or until they are tender when pierced with a fork. Using a slotted spoon, transfer the leeks to a kitchen towel to drain, cut side down.

TO MAKE THE VINAIGRETTE

In a small bowl, whisk together the vinegar, salt and pepper to taste, and mustard until they start to emulsify. Slowly pour in the olive oil, whisking until the mixture becomes creamy.

TO ASSEMBLE

In a small bowl, toss the egg with the parsley.

Arrange the leeks on a small platter or on individual plates with the white tips facing one direction. Drizzle the vinaigrette over the leeks and scatter the parsley and egg mixture over the white tips. Place a sliver of anchovy over the chopped egg and parsley mixture.

SERVES 6

Wild Mushroom Risotto with Truffles

1 ounce dried porcini mushrooms

5 tablespoons unsalted butter

1½ pounds fresh wild mushrooms (such as porcini, chanterelles, oyster, shiitake, or morels) cleaned, trimmed, and uniformly sliced into dime-sized pieces (use cremini mushrooms in the absence of wild mushrooms)

5 to 8 cups chicken stock, preferably homemade

4 shallots, the size of a quarter, minced

2 tablespoons fresh chopped thyme leaves

1½ cups Carnaroli rice, or whatever equivalent is available

½ cup dry red wine, such as Chianti, or white wine

¼ cup mascarpone or heavy whipping cream

¾ cup freshly grated Parmigiano-Reggiano cheese

2 tablespoons chopped parsley

1 ounce fresh white or black truffles (totally optional but totally worth it)

This is a wonderfully woodsy, aromatic risotto, brought to the heavens with truffles scraped on top, but still delightful without. You cannot be in a hurry with risotto. This is the type of dinner you want to have with good friends who will join you in the kitchen as you stir.

There is much debate about the best rice to use for risotto but after much consensus taking and experimentation, I advise Carnaroli for creaminess and Baldo for the way it holds up, or Arborio. But besides the attentiveness required for stirring and allowing each addition of broth to be absorbed before more is added, another bit of patience is required at the end of the stirring process. That is waiting. Waiting once the heat is turned off for the risotto to catch up to itself, allowing it to rest for a few minutes before serving.

During late autumn and early winter, truffle season is one of the great experiences of living in France, where you can find both the local black truffles and the white ones imported from Italy. Fortunately, you can buy them in the States, too (see Sources, page 217). I know most of us are don't have access to them much of the time, but when you do, shave them with abandon on this risotto. I do not recommend using truffle oil in place of a fresh truffle.

Soak the porcini in 1 cup of very hot water for 30 minutes or longer. Strain the liquid through a paper coffee filter or cheesecloth into a small bowl and set aside. Chop the porcini and set aside.

Heat a large skillet over medium-high heat and add 2 tablespoons of the butter. When it sizzles, add all the mushrooms (wild and reconstituted porcini), and cook, stirring gently while the mushrooms simmer, at first giving off their juices, and then reabsorbing them, 5 to 8 minutes. Set the mushrooms aside and keep warm.

In a large pot, bring the chicken stock and the reserved porcini broth to a boil, then let it simmer on a burner at the back of the stove.

In a large, heavy skillet, melt 2 tablespoons of the butter. Add the shallots and cook until they become translucent, about 3 minutes, stirring as you go. Add the thyme and stir again.

Add the rice, stirring so that all the grains are coated and hot, about 3 minutes. Add the wine and stir until it evaporates.

Add a ladle (about ½ cup) of the simmering stock and stir until it is almost absorbed. Continue adding a ladle of the broth at a time, stirring continuously, until it is used up. It will take 18 to 23 minutes for Carnaroli rice and a little longer for Arborio. Taste as you go and make sure that there is not a chalky taste to the grain and that the rice is substantially creamy.

Add the mushrooms, the remaining tablespoon of butter, and the cream, and stir. Scatter most of the cheese over the top and stir gently, saving a little cheese to top the final dish. Remove the pot from the heat and allow it to rest for at least 3 minutes.

Transfer the risotto to a warm bowl, sprinkle a little chopped parsley on top, and serve at the table with the truffle and a truffle slicer alongside.

SERVES 6

FRISÉE SALAD WITH LARDONS

This is one of my favorite French salads. Frisée is a curly chicory or endive that is bittersweet and tender. Lardons are little dices of bacon, fried to a crispy crunch, that are tossed with the frisée in this traditional bistro salad. If you are not fond of frisée, use another lettuce, such as escarole.

Tear the frisée into bite-sized pieces and place in a salad bowl. Refrigerate until ready to use.

In a skillet cook the bacon over medium heat until it is light brown and crisp. Drain on paper towels.

Combine the garlic, vinegar, and salt and pepper to taste in a small bowl. Add the olive oil and whisk to incorporate. Toss the dressing with the frisée and sprinkle the bacon over the top.

SERVES 6

2 heads frisée lettuce, washed and dried

4 to 6 slices thick-cut, bacon, diced

1 clove garlic, minced

2 tablespoons red wine vinegar

Salt and freshly ground black pepper

6 tablespoons extra-virgin olive oil

PEARS POACHED IN RED WINE WITH SPICES

6 firm pears, such as Bosc

1 bottle dry red wine, such as Pinot Noir

¾ cup sugar

6 to 8 black peppercorns

1 cinnamon stick

1 clove

2 cardamom pods, or a few seeds

1 star anise

3-inch strip of orange zest, white pith removed

Crème fraîche or vanilla ice cream

This refreshingly simple dessert is perfect after the risotto or any rich meal. It can be made ahead of time, getting more intensely flavored as the pears steep in their juices. Serve with Sue Moore's Cardamom Cookies (page 139) or bakery-bought small palmiers or madeleines.

Slice the bottoms off the pears so that they will stand flat. With an apple corer, remove the core (from the bottom). Peel the pears, leaving on the stem.

In a saucepan that will hold all the pears standing up, gently warm the wine and sugar over low heat until the sugar dissolves. Then add all the spices and the orange zest and warm for a few minutes over medium heat to meld the flavors.

Add the pears, flat bottom down, and lower the heat to simmer the pears for 20 to 25 minutes, basting them several times. The pears are done when they are slightly tender when pierced with a sharp knife, but still firm enough to hold their shape. Turn off the heat and allow the pears to cool in their juices. The sauce will thicken as it cools.

Transfer the pears and sauce to a shallow bowl. Spoon the sauce over the top of the pears. Serve warm or at room temperature, with a dollop of crème fraîche or vanilla ice cream.

SERVES 6

A CLASSIC
PARISIAN SUPPER

Italian Salami or French Sausage with Cherry Tomatoes

· · · · ·

Belgian Endive and Ham Gratin

· · · · ·

Green Beans Sautéed with Wild Mushrooms

· · · · ·

Red and Green Salad
(PAGE 27)

· · · · ·

Succulent Prunes with Armagnac and Crème Fraîche

· · · · ·

Sue Moore's Cardamom Cookies

When I first started giving parties in Paris I thought I had to have lots of courses—a starter, a fish, a meat, a vegetable, a potato dish—salad, cheeses, and dessert. My friend Daniel Le Clercq, who knows a lot about the French table, dispelled all of that. In complimenting me on my dinners, he made me feel as if I had permission to do whatever I wanted as long as it tasted good and followed certain prejudices of his and mine (see Introduction). So when I last invited him for dinner and asked what he would like me to make, he suggested the same dish that is a favorite of another friend who was coming that night as well— Belgian endive and ham gratin. I had forgotten about this sophisticated, reassuring combination.

The gratin of endive wrapped in ham and bubbling brown with melted cheese is one of those old-fashioned recipes that deserves to be revisited. It's satisfying, rich, and stands on its own as a simple main course for an informal supper. It would be a good choice to serve after a cocktail party for guests who stay late.

Offer a plate of dry sliced Italian salami or French sausage as an hors d'oeuvre, along with a small bowl of cherry tomatoes. I like to serve the gratin with a simple starter such as haricots verts with mushrooms (avoid another dish in a cream sauce) and a crisp green salad. Present one perfectly ripe cheese with the salad and end with a succulent prune compote served with tiny cardamom cookies.

PARTY PLAN

THE DAY BEFORE

- Soak the prunes and make the compote

DAY OF THE PARTY

- Prepare the components of the gratin
- Steam the green beans
- Prepare the mushrooms
- Prepare the salad
- Make the cookies

DECORATING IDEAS

Lay a branch of persimmons or pomegranates in the center of the table. Or make an arrangement of green and black grapes, then put tangerines, small apples, pears, persimmons, and pomegranates around the grapes.

Belgian Endive and Ham Gratin

FOR THE ENDIVE

1 teaspoon salt

8 heads medium-sized Belgian endive (if large, cut in half lengthwise)

8 thin slices boiled ham (each large enough to wrap one endive)

¾ cup grated Gruyère or Swiss cheese

FOR THE BÉCHAMEL SAUCE

2½ to 3 cups milk, warmed

2 tablespoons unsalted butter

3 tablespoons flour

½ cup finely grated Parmesan cheese

Salt and freshly ground white pepper

This rich and creamy gratin is a great party dish, as it can be prepared in advance and heated in the oven just before you sit down. Cooking the endive removes some of its inherent bitterness, but it still maintains its integrity of shape and taste.

Preheat the oven to 375°F. Grease the sides and bottom of a baking or gratin dish large enough to hold 8 endives.

TO PREPARE THE ENDIVE

Bring a pot of salted water to a boil. Drop the endives into the boiling water and cook for 15 to 20 minutes or until tender when pierced with the blade of a sharp knife. Drain well.

TO MAKE THE SAUCE

While the endives are cooking, make the sauce: In a saucepan, warm the milk over low heat. Set aside.

In a heavy saucepan, warm the butter over low heat. When it starts to froth, add the flour, salt and pepper, whisking constantly until it thickens. Pour in 2½ cups of the milk in a steady stream, whisking constantly until it is smooth. If the sauce seems too thick, add some more of the milk.

Reduce the heat to a simmer and cook the sauce until it thickens, 10 to 15 minutes, whisking constantly. Whisk in the Parmesan cheese to incorporate. Remove from the heat and keep warm on the back of the stove.

TO ASSEMBLE

When the endives are cool enough to handle, cut off the tough cores and wrap each one in a slice of ham. Place the endives, seam side down in the baking dish and pour the béchamel over the top. Scatter the Gruyère cheese over the sauce. (If you are making the gratin in advance, it can be refrigerated, then brought to room temperature before baking.)

Bake for 20 to 25 minutes or until the surface is bubbly. Put under the broiler to brown the top. Serve in the baking dish at the table.

SERVES 4 TO 6

Green Beans Sautéed with Wild Mushrooms

I love the delicate, French haricots verts, buts if you can't find them, use small green beans. Julia Child always suggested cooking them in massive amounts of water, or you can steam them, if you prefer. Americans tend to like a bit of crunch to their beans while the French generally prefer them cooked a little more; I like them somewhere in between.

Bring a large pot of salted water to a boil.

Meanwhile, heat the butter and the olive oil in a large skillet over medium heat. Add the garlic and cook for 1 minute, or until it becomes translucent. Add the mushrooms, cooking them until they give off their juices and then reabsorb them, 5 to 7 minutes. Season with salt and pepper to taste. Keep the mushrooms warm on the stovetop.

Add the beans to the boiling water and cook for 3 to 5 minutes, or until slightly tender (haricots verts will take less time than green beans). Drain.

Transfer about half of the mushrooms to a small dish and keep warm. Add the beans to the mushrooms in the skillet and stir to combine. Mound the beans and mushrooms gently on a serving platter and top with the reserved mushrooms. Season again with salt and pepper.

SERVES 6

3 tablespoons unsalted butter

1 tablespoon extra-virgin olive oil

1 clove garlic, minced

½ pound chanterelles or other wild mushrooms, cleaned and cut into bite-sized pieces

Salt and freshly ground black pepper

1½ pounds haricots verts or green beans, trimmed

SUCCULENT PRUNES WITH ARMAGNAC AND CRÈME FRAÎCHE

1 pound pitted prunes

1 large piece of orange zest, 1 inch by 3 inches

2-inch section of fresh ginger, unpeeled

2 cups Lapsang Souchong, Earl Grey, or other hot brewed tea

½ cup sugar

Juice of 1 large orange

2 cinnamon sticks

½ cup Armagnac or cognac

1 cup crème fraîche

Prune compote is a tasty choice for an undemanding dessert, and it can be made well in advance and warmed at the last minute. I learned from a French neighbor to plump prunes in a smoky tea such as Lapsang Souchong and then to stew them gently in sugar and spices with a splash of Armagnac. You can store any leftovers in a jar in the refrigerator for up to two weeks. They can be made on the spot, of course, but it is money in the bank to have a stash of these little jewels in your refrigerator, ready to go with a spoonful of crème fraîche, sour cream, vanilla ice cream, or thick Greek yogurt on top.

Place the prunes, orange zest, and ginger in a nonreactive saucepan and pour the tea over them. Soak for at least 1 hour or overnight. Pour off all but about ⅓ cup of the tea from the prunes. Add the sugar, orange juice, cinnamon sticks, ½ cup water, and the Armagnac. Simmer over low heat for 10 to 15 minutes. Remove the ginger.

Spoon the prunes into small ramekins or dessert bowls and serve with a dab of crème fraîche on top. Serve with cardamom cookies (recipe follows).

SERVES 6 TO 8

SUE MOORE'S CARDAMOM COOKIES

My friend Sue Moore does a lot of things well. She is an expert tennis player, an environmentalist, a CPA to many people in the food world, and an experienced forager. When I invite her for dinner, I always hope she will bring along a couple of chilled rolls of cardamom cookie dough. Sue slices and cooks one roll as we have our salad and usually leaves the other roll in the freezer for me. I think this is the ideal present for a guest to bring to a dinner party. These tiny, brittle cookies are exceptional. They have an elegant look and a surprising bite from the cardamom seeds. (Sue suggests that buying cardamom seeds from an Indian spice shop is less expensive than buying them at a fancy food store.)

In a large bowl, combine the butter, sugars, egg, and vanilla and beat until light and fluffy. Sift the flour and baking soda into the mixture and mix well. Stir in the cardamom seeds. Shape the dough into two 10-inch logs the diameter of a quarter. Wrap the logs in waxed paper or parchment and chill for at least an hour.

Preheat the oven to 350°F.

Cut the logs into very thin slices, about ¼ inch thick, and place on ungreased baking sheets. Bake for about 10 minutes or until golden brown. Watch carefully, they can burn easily.

Transfer the cookies to a wire rack after they've cooled for a few minutes.

MAKES 60 TO 70 COOKIES

1 cup (2 sticks) unsalted butter, softened

1 cup confectioners' sugar

½ cup granulated sugar

1 large egg

2 teaspoons vanilla

2¼ cups all-purpose flour

½ teaspoon baking soda

1 teaspoon black cardamom seeds

An Old-Fashioned Family Thanksgiving

Crab Legs on Endive with Homemade Mayonnaise

· · · · ·

Sage-Roasted, Dry-Brined Turkey

· · · · ·

Mississippi-Style Corn Bread Stuffing

· · · · ·

Browned Brussels Sprouts with Pancetta

· · · · ·

Rum-Baked Sweet Potatoes

· · · · ·

Baked Persimmon Pudding

Sage-Roasted, Dry-Brined Turkey

Remember when everyone was brining turkey in huge pots of seasoned water? It might have tasted good, but it was hard to find a spot to keep the turkey cold during the brining process. Brining poultry provides better texture, moisture, and flavor. Here is a simpler and equally delicious way to brine the bird in the refrigerator. Order a fresh, organic, free-range turkey well in advance of your celebration. You want a big bird, no matter how many guests you have invited, so that there will be plenty of leftovers. I am not a gravy fan, but if you are, by all means make some.

TO DRY BRINE THE TURKEY

Two to three days before cooking, unwrap the turkey and rinse it well. Splash a little whisky in the cavity to get rid of any lurking aromas. Pat dry with paper towels. Take a handful of salt and sprinkle it generously all over the bird, under the wings, and in the cavity. Wrap the bird in kitchen towels or plastic wrap and refrigerate for 2 to 3 days, until a few of hours before baking time. Allow the turkey to come to room temperature before stuffing it.

TO COOK THE TURKEY

Prepare the stuffing as directed. Stuff the bird at the last minute or put the stuffing in a shallow dish and bake it.

Preheat the oven to 450°F.

Place the stuffed turkey in a large roasting pan and dot with the butter. Cook for about 45 minutes, then reduce the temperature to 375°F and continue to cook the turkey for another 3 hours. Baste the turkey with the pan drippings every 30 to 45 minutes. If it gets too brown, put a tent of foil over it.

When the leg wiggles freely or the inner thigh provides a reading of 180°F with an instant-read thermometer, the bird is done. Remove it from the oven and place it on a platter or cutting board with a lip so that the juices will not spill. Allow it to rest for about half an hour before carving.

SERVES AT LEAST 12

One 18-pound fresh, organic, free-range turkey

Sea salt

4 tablespoons unsalted butter

Mississippi-Style Corn Bread Stuffing (page 144)

MISSISSIPPI-STYLE CORN BREAD STUFFING

FOR THE CORN BREAD

2 cups all-purpose flour

1½ cups cornmeal

1 teaspoon salt

2 tablespoons baking powder

½ cup sugar

2 large eggs, well beaten

2 cups milk

½ cup bacon drippings or melted unsalted butter

FOR THE STUFFING

8 to 10 cups crumbled corn bread

½ cup chopped flat-leaf parsley

6 tablespoons chopped fresh herbs in any combination (sage, oregano, savory, thyme) or 4 tablespoons of the dried herbs

A few sprigs celery leaves, chopped

Sea salt and freshly ground black pepper

3 tablespoons rendered bacon fat or unsalted butter

2 medium yellow onions, chopped

4 ribs celery, thinly sliced

1 to 1½ cups chicken or turkey broth

My mother's family came from Mississippi, where they use a lot of bacon fat in their cooking. For special occasions and for remarkably good taste, I use it for my corn bread stuffing. If you prefer, you can use butter instead. The hardest part of making this corn bread is resisting the temptation to eat it hot with butter and jam.

TO MAKE THE CORN BREAD

Preheat the oven to 425°F. Grease a 10 x 13-inch baking dish.

In a medium-sized bowl, combine the flour, cornmeal, salt, baking powder, and sugar and stir well. Add the eggs, milk, and bacon drippings, stir well again and pour into the prepared dish.

Bake for about 20 minutes, or until the corn bread is golden brown on the top. Let it cool.

TO MAKE THE STUFFING

Place the crumbled corn bread in a large bowl. Add the parsley, herbs, celery leaves, and salt and pepper to taste and mix well.

Heat the bacon fat in a large skillet over medium heat. Add the onions and celery; sauté for about 10 minutes. Fold the onion mixture into the corn bread mixture. Add enough broth to moisten the stuffing to your liking.

Stuff the neck and turkey cavity. Any extra stuffing can be cooked in an ovenproof dish, loosely covered, for about 20 minutes at 350°F. If you prefer your stuffing on the crisp side, do not cover it.

BROWNED BRUSSELS SPROUTS WITH PANCETTA

Believe it or not, even children love these winter vegetables. There is something about slicing them, browning them, and giving them a boost with pancetta that makes these Brussels sprouts quite alluring. If you have vegetarians at your table, omit the pancetta.

Bring a large pot of salted water to a boil. Trim the tough ends of the Brussels sprouts. Cut them in half lengthwise; if they are large, quarter them lengthwise. Blanch the Brussels sprouts for about 8 minutes in the boiling water, and drain.

Heat the olive oil over medium-high heat in a skillet large enough to hold all the Brussels sprouts (or use two skillets). Add the pancetta and cook for about 3 minutes. Add the Brussels sprouts and cook until they become nicely browned and slightly caramelized on the cut side, 10 to 15 minutes. Stir and season with salt and pepper to taste.

This dish can be made ahead of time and will reheat nicely; but ideally, it is best cooked at the last minute.

SERVES 8 TO 12

2 pounds Brussels sprouts

2 tablespoons extra-virgin olive oil

4 ounces pancetta or bacon, cut into ½ inch pieces

Sea salt and freshly ground black pepper

Rum-Baked Sweet Potatoes

4 to 5 pounds sweet potatoes
or yams

2 oranges

1 cup dark brown sugar

⅓ cup dark rum, preferably Meyers

Salt and freshly ground
black pepper

8 tablespoons (1 stick) unsalted
butter, cut into small pieces

While I don't like the expression "comfort food," I must admit this dish is comforting and colorful and just delicious (without marshmallows!).

Preheat the oven to 400°F.

Prick the sweet potatoes with a fork and place them on a baking sheet. Bake for about an hour or until tender when pierced with a fork. Remove from the oven; when they are cool enough to handle, scoop out the flesh.

In a large bowl, mash the potatoes. It's all right if there are some lumps, the mixture does not have to be a fine puree.

With a rasp grater or a citrus zester, remove the zest of both oranges, chop it and set aside. (Using these implements reduces the risk of getting the bitter white pith of the orange along with the zest.) Juice the oranges, then strain the juice, pouring it into the potatoes. Add half the zest, half the brown sugar, and half the rum. Season to taste with salt and pepper. Transfer the mixture to a casserole dish you can bring to the table. (The dish may be prepared in advance to this point and refrigerated. Bring it to room temperature and bake for about 20 minutes at 350°F.)

Dot the top with the butter. Sprinkle the remaining brown sugar and rum over the top. Bake until heated through, about 30 minutes. Just before serving, scatter the remaining zest over the top.

SERVES 8 TO 12

BAKED PERSIMMON PUDDING

A takeoff on a traditional English steamed pudding, this persimmon pudding is baked, rather than steamed. To my mind, it is the absolute perfect ending to this big holiday feast. It is deep, dark, rich, and dense. tasting more of persimmons than spice. This pudding is made with acorn-shaped Hachiya persimmons, pointed at one end. They ripen to a soft gelatinous pulp, making them excellent for baking. If your persimmons are not dead ripe, freeze them solid; as they defrost they will ripen and lose their bitterness.

Preheat the oven to 350°F. Butter an 11 inch round Pyrex pie plate.

Sift the flour, baking powder, baking soda, cinnamon, and salt together onto a piece of waxed paper or into a small bowl.

Cut the persimmons in half and scrape the pulp into the bowl of a food processor. Pulse until they form a puree. Add the flour mixture and pulse until combined. Add the sugar, milk, cream, honey, and vanilla. Pulse to combine.

Melt the butter in a small saucepan over medium heat until it begins to brown, then pour it into the bowl of the food processor. Pulse again to combine.

Pour the batter into the prepared pan. Bake for about 2½ to 3 hours, or until the pudding is set and deep dark brown on the surface. It will not be fluffy, but rather flat in appearance.

Serve warm or at room temperature, with whipped cream, if desired.

SERVES 8 TO 12

2 to 3 pounds ripe Hachiya persimmons

1⅓ cups all-purpose flour

½ teaspoon baking powder

½ teaspoon baking soda

Pinch of cinnamon

Pinch of sea salt

1 cup sugar

1½ cups whole milk

½ cup whipping cream

1 tablespoon honey

1 tablespoon vanilla extract

8 tablespoons (1 stick) unsalted butter

Whipped cream for topping, optional

A Romantic Dinner for Two

Caviar and Crème Fraîche on Cornmeal Blini

· · · · ·

Alice B. Toklas Chicken

· · · · ·

Roasted Sage Potatoes

· · · · ·

Garlicky Spinach Sauté

· · · · ·

Crispy-Creamy Chocolate Cookies

When I returned from Paris to see if romance was in the stars with the man with whom I had been carrying on an electronic epistolary relationship in San Francisco, I decided to lure him to my house and seduce him with the oldest trick I knew—my cooking. My good-luck recipe, Alice B. Toklas Chicken, had worked in the past. I was sure the aromas of this mahogany chicken with port and orange would captivate him the moment he walked in the door. Toklas served a version of this recipe to the writers and artists of the Parisian salons she held with Gertrude Stein; her guests kept coming back. I was hoping this recipe would have the same effect, and it did.

Absolutely everything can be set up ahead of time for this meal, so you don't have to spend so much time in the kitchen. The romantic caviar tray can be arranged to go alongside a cooler for champagne, and the chicken and potatoes can be popped in the oven an hour before you eat. As for the menu, the combination of the tastes and textures of caviar and cornmeal is sublime. The garlicky spinach dish provides a splash of color to the meal and can be warmed on the stovetop a couple of minutes before the chicken comes out of the oven. The chocolate cookies are seductively rich.

Most significantly, this menu isn't filling so you will feel like romance.

DINNER PLAN

DAY OF THE DINNER

- Make the blini
- Salt the chicken
- Wash the spinach
- Make the cookies
- Set a tray with two champagne glasses and put a bottle of champagne on ice. Prepare another small tray alongside with the caviar setup.

DECORATING IDEAS

Light lots of candles and arrange bouquets of roses in the dining room.

Caviar and Crème Fraîche on Cornmeal Blini

FOR THE BLINI

¼ cup cornmeal

¼ cup all-purpose flour

1 teaspoon sugar

½ cup crème fraîche or buttermilk

½ teaspoon baking powder

¼ teaspoon salt

2 large eggs

¼ cup melted unsalted butter

FOR THE CAVIAR SETUP

2 ounces caviar

¼ cup crème fraîche or sour cream

1 tablespoon chopped chives

Something magical happens in the mouth when the tiny caviar eggs burst as you roll them around with the even tinier grains of cornmeal. The blini are the size of silver dollars—you will only need about three per person, but if this dinner is truly romantic, perhaps the extra batter will come in handy for breakfast the next morning.

TO MAKE THE BLINI

In a medium bowl, whisk together the cornmeal, flour, sugar, crème fraîche, salt, eggs, and 2 tablespoons of the melted butter.

Place a heavy skillet preferable a well seasoned iron one, on medium-high heat and add the remaining 2 tablespoons of melted butter. Drop about a tablespoon or so of batter into the skillet for each blini, they should be the size of silver dollars. Cook as you would pancakes, until they brown on one side, then turn to cook the other side. Save the extra batter for pancakes if you like.

Transfer the blini to a small plate and keep warm, on top of the stove, or serve at room temperature. To serve, place a dab of crème fraîche on each blini and top it with a little caviar. Sprinkle the chives on top.

SERVES 2

ALICE B. TOKLAS CHICKEN

1 medium-sized (about 3½ pounds) roasting chicken, preferably free-range

Salt

2 tablespoons unsalted butter

2 tablespoons extra-virgin olive oil

½ cup ruby port

½ cup orange juice

3 tablespoons heavy cream

Zest of 1 orange, grated

Salt and freshly ground black pepper

One wintry day I picked up The Alice B. Toklas Cookbook, hoping to soothe the monotony of the long gray season with something inspired and Parisian to cook. I was delighted to find a recipe that my mother had served at dinner parties. Later it became one of my most requested dishes when I was a young caterer in San Francisco. Alice B. Toklas called it Katie's Capon, but I always make it with chicken. This recipe is adapted for the American kitchen.

When you bring the chicken home from the market, unwrap it and sprinkle it generously with salt. Cover and refrigerate it until ready to cook. Bring the bird to room temperature before cooking. Do not rub off the salt.

Preheat the oven to 400°F.

In a large ovenproof skillet warm the butter and olive oil over medium heat. Brown the chicken breast side down, for 3 to 5 minutes then turn it over and brown the other side for 3 to 5 minutes.

Place the skillet in the oven and roast the chicken for 45 minutes. Pour the port over the chicken and baste it. Roast for 10 minutes more, than add the orange juice and baste again. Roast for about 5 minutes more. The chicken is done when the juices of the thigh run clear when pierced with the blade of a sharp knife, or when the thigh wiggles easily. Remove the chicken from the oven, transfer it to a cutting board, and let it rest as you make the sauce.

Skim as much fat off the top of the juices in the skillet as you can and discard. Place the skillet over medium heat and add the cream, stirring up the crispy bits on the bottom. Add about half the orange zest and allow the sauce to reduce as you stir constantly for a few minutes.

Carve the chicken and transfer it to a serving platter. Pour some of the sauce over the chicken and transfer the rest into a gravy boat or small pitcher and serve it at the table. Sprinkle the remaining orange zest over the chicken.

SERVES 2 TO 4

Alice B. Toklas Is Back

Alice B. Toklas has haunted me for years. Her recipes were the mainstay of my young married days and of my catering business. I think of her every time I drive past her pre-1906-earthquake house not far from mine in San Francisco. And just recently, I was walking up Rue de Fleurus, around the corner from where I live in Paris, and I noticed a plaque on the building declaring that Gertrude Stein (and Alice B. Toklas) had once lived there. When I mentioned this to one of my favorite cooks in Paris, he told me he had been rereading and cooking from *The Alice B. Toklas Cookbook*. I couldn't wait to get home and dig out my dog-eared copy. Something was in the air.

And then, coincidentally, as I was leafing through the book, another friend called to invite me to an exhibition at the San Francisco Public Library—"We Love You, Alice B. Toklas." The literary muse, cook, and hostess to the most legendary writers and artists of early-20th-century Paris was captured in photographs, chic as could be, in furs and feathers and a big black mustache. It was a tribute to the woman whose humor and creativity afforded her the role of consummate hostess to the most fascinating people of artistic Paris—Hemingway, Picasso, Matisse, Paul Bowles, and Braque.

Later I read that during WWI she and Gertrude Stein delivered medical supplies—5,000 thermometers—to French and American soldiers. And during the Nazi occupation the two Jewish women survived upon the generosity of the villagers in the provincial towns where they lived. Resourceful recipes and wild stories of these times are chronicled in her cookbook.

It is amazing how her recipes have survived. The cookbook was first published in 1954, giving her a certain celebrity (largely due to the hashish fudge recipe). Later, in the 1970s, a board member of the San Francisco Museum of Modern Art asked me and my catering partner to prepare a dinner before the opening of the Gertrude Stein collection. The hostess asked us to make brownies, leaving out the hashish, of course. We would not have dreamed of using the drug for such an event. But many of them assumed we did and came into the kitchen accusing us of purposely getting them high!

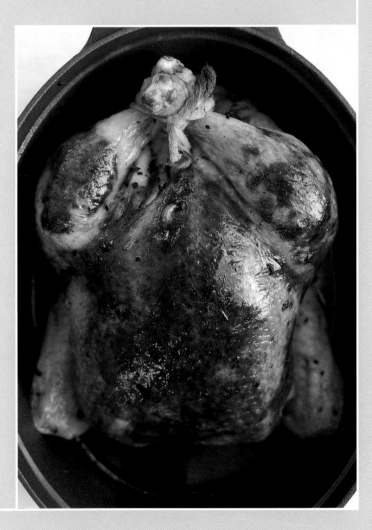

Roasted Sage Potatoes

8 to 10 small fingerling potatoes, or 2 russets cut into eighths

2 tablespoons extra-virgin olive oil

1 tablespoon unsalted butter, melted

4 sage leaves

Sea salt and freshly ground black pepper

These potatoes go well with the creamy sauce of the chicken dish, and are roasted during the last 15 minutes the chicken is in the oven, which imparts some extra flavor.

Preheat the oven to 400°F.

Bring a medium-sized pot of salted water to a boil. Add the potatoes and cook for 10 minutes or until tender when pierced with a fork. Drain.

Pour the olive oil and butter into a small baking dish. Add the potatoes and crumble the sage over the top. Season generously with salt and pepper and toss well. Bake for about 15 minutes, until crisp and tender.

SERVES 2 TO 4

Garlicky Spinach Sauté

3 to 4 tablespoons pine nuts

3 tablespoons extra-virgin olive oil

2 cloves garlic, minced

2 pounds tender spinach, washed, stemmed, and roughly chopped

3 tablespoons currants or small raisins

Salt and freshly ground black pepper

There is something irresistible about the classic Mediterranean combination of spinach, pine nuts, and currants. It's sweet and crunchy and ever so slightly bitter. You can make this dish a little ahead of time and warm it gently (with a little extra water), at the last moment. Be sure to wash the spinach at least twice, if not three times.

Heat a small, heavy skillet over medium-high heat. Add the pine nuts and cook them for about a minute, shaking the pan constantly, until they are a bit crisp and aromatic but not brown. Transfer to a small bowl.

Heat the olive oil in a large, heavy skillet over medium-high heat, add the garlic, and cook just until it becomes translucent, about 1 minute. Add the spinach and cook, stirring, until it wilts, 3 to 5 minutes. Stir in the currants. Season with salt and pepper to taste, and stir in the pine nuts at the last minute.

SERVES 2 TO 4

CRISPY-CREAMY CHOCOLATE COOKIES

These chocolate cookies, crisp on the outside and creamy inside, are an adaptation of a Pierre Hermé (the famous Parisian baker) chocolate cookie. Once rolled into logs and wrapped, the dough keeps for 3 days in the refrigerator and can be frozen for up to a month.

Sift together the cocoa powder, baking soda, and flour. In a large mixing bowl, using a mixer, cream the butter until smooth, add the brown sugar and granulated sugar and blend again. Add the salt and vanilla and blend for about 1½ minutes. Add the flour mixture to the butter mixture and mix on the lowest speed until the ingredients are incorporated. The dough will be crumbly. Stir in the chopped chocolate.

Turn the dough onto a work surface. Press the mixture together with your hands, forming a ball. Cut the ball in half and work each half into a log about 1½ inches in diameter. Wrap each log in plastic and refrigerate for at least 1 hour.

Preheat the oven to 325°F. Line 2 baking sheets with parchment.

Slice the logs into ½-inch-thick rounds. Place the rounds on the baking sheets, 1 inch apart. If the cookies break apart, press them back together.

Bake one sheet at a time for 12 minutes. The cookies will not be firm nor appear to be done. Remove them from the oven and let them cool on the sheet on a wire rack until they are barely warm. Store the cookies in an airtight container.

MAKES 4 DOZEN COOKIES

⅓ cup excellent-quality processed, sweetened cocoa powder, such as E. Guittard or Scharffen Berger

½ teaspoon baking soda

¼ cup all-purpose flour

11 tablespoons (1 stick plus 3 tablespoons) unsalted butter

⅔ cup dark brown sugar

¼ cup granulated sugar

¼ teaspoon sea salt or fleur de sel

1 teaspoon vanilla extract

5 ounces excellent-quality bittersweet chocolate (such as E. Guittard), roughly chopped

COCKTAIL PARTIES AND BENEFITS

FOR COCKTAIL PARTIES

Roasted Asparagus with Aioli

· · · · ·

Crab Legs on Endive with
Homemade Mayonnaise
(PAGE 142)

· · · · ·

Taramasalata and Smoked Salmon Toasts
(PAGE 40)

· · · · ·

Cucumber Rounds with Smoked Trout
and Horseradish Cream
(PAGE 190)

· · · · ·

Double-Decker Caviar Cake

· · · · ·

Seed-and-Herb-Crusted
Pork Tenderloin
(PAGE 191)

FOR BENEFITS

Assorted Nuts and Olives

· · · · ·

Frittata of Chard with Melted Fontina

· · · · ·

Wicker Basket Stuffed with Seasonal
Vegetables and Warm Bagna Cauda
(PAGE 106)

· · · · ·

Cecelia Chiang's Minced Chicken
in Lettuce Cups

· · · · ·

Platter of Fresh Fruit and Cheeses

· · · · ·

Parmesan-Pine Nut Crackers
(PAGE 52)

· · · · ·

Assortment of Cookies
(recipes throughout the book or bakery cookies such as macaroons,
Mexican wedding cookies, small palmiers, meringues)

· · · · ·

Flourless Chocolate Nest Cake

The best thing about my mother was her political activism. I was brought up helping to cook for all sorts of benefits for her social issues. She insisted, "People want to know that their donations are going to the cause and not the food they are being served." With that in mind, I offer suggestions for a lively buffet of colorful dishes that will tide people over and encourage them to dig deep into their pockets.

A cocktail party can be more lavish than a benefit, or give the appearance of extravagance. A greater variety of drink and food is in order, the decorations can be elaborate, and you might choose to have help, in the kitchen, for serving, and at the bar.

PARTY PLAN

For more general tips about party giving, please consult the Introduction.

THE DAY OF THE PARTY

- Arrange flowers, organize the table and bar
- If the party is a benefit, ask someone to help with the greeting table and take money
- Have plenty of cocktail napkins
- Organize helpers
- Prepare everything in advance
- Give yourself time to relax before the party so you can be the best possible host

DECORATING IDEAS

For festive parties position a metallic cloth (silver for the holidays, copper for fall) on top of a neutral-colored cloth. Then run votives or candlesticks down the length of the table. The metallic cloth reflects the light of the candles and provides festive sparkle. To go all out, take long lengths of wire ribbon in metallic or silk and coil them loosely around the candlesticks or votives.

Then make a splash with an unusual eye-catching edible centerpiece. One dramatic ingredient simply flaunted makes a big impression.

What to Serve

Carve out your own style party using some of these recipes as ideas and add your own twist. Although I've given separate menus for benefits and cocktail parties, all the benefit recipes are suitable for cocktail parties, and you can certainly mix and match to suit your soirée and your budget.

I always think it is a good idea to have an item from every food group on a buffet, so there is something for everyone. Vegetables are covered with the vegetable basket or the asparagus. Consider serving an assortment of artisanal cheeses to go with the easy-to-eat fruit. For meat, prepare medallions of pork with a balsamic drizzle, and crab legs on endive leaves for fish. Place nuts, olives, and even good salt-vinegar potato chips around the rooms in pretty bowls.

For a purely social cocktail party, make a caviar cake with salmon eggs as a stunning centerpiece. Then, depending upon how substantial you want the food to be, serve lettuce leaves filled with Cecelia Chaing's Chinese Chicken. A seasonal frittata, cut into bite-sized pieces is always good. Crostini are an appetizing stand-up party choice. The fanciful chocolate nest cake is dramatic and delicious for any ocasion. It will require a separate plate and fork.

The Bar

Set up a bar with lots of ice, sparkling water, and one very good red and white wine. Have ⅔ white wine to ⅓ red. Offer a sparkling wine such as an Italian Prosecco or a good champagne. White wine is a good idea if you have rugs or furniture that you worry about with spills. You could have a bottle or two of chilled vodka or other liquor. Keep it simple, guests do not need lots of beverage choice. Figure on at least a half bottle of wine per person for a short party, more if the party is long. Since many people like to alternate alcoholic drinks with sparkling water or only drink sparkling water, provide at least a half bottle of sparkling water per person.

Have plenty of glasses sparkling in the candlelight on a handsome crisp tablecloth. You'll need an ice bucket with ice for water and mixed drinks, also a cooler filled with at least 20 pounds of ice to chill the wine, vodka, or sparkling wine. Have lime or lemon wedges arranged in a bowl.

FRITTATA OF CHARD WITH MELTED FONTINA

5 tablespoons extra-virgin olive oil

1 medium onion, chopped

2 cloves garlic, minced

2 bunches chard, washed

10 large eggs

¼ cup heavy cream

Salt and freshly ground
black pepper

3 ounces Fontina cheese, sliced
into small pieces

Frittatas are versatile. The ingredients for this Italian/Californian dish can vary throughout the year—Swiss chard and kale in the fall and winter, fava beans and baby artichokes in the spring, zucchini and pattypan squash in the summer, and roasted red or yellow (peeled) peppers in the fall. Frittatas are good hot out of the oven or served at room temperature. They go well with a simple green salad and crusty bread for lunch or supper, too.

Preheat the oven to 350°F.

In a large deep pot, heat 2 tablespoons of the olive oil over medium heat. Add the onion and garlic and sauté just until the onions become translucent, about 3 minutes. Season with salt and pepper to taste.

Meanwhile, loosely chop the chard, slicing the stems into small pieces. Add the stems to the onion mixture and cook for about 10 minutes, or until tender. If the stems seem a little tough, add a splash of water to quicken the cooking time (let the water cook down). Add the chard leaves, a few handfuls at a time, and continue to cook, stirring occasionally and tossing with tongs until tender, 8 to 10 minutes. Set aside.

In a bowl, beat together the eggs, cream, and salt and pepper to taste. Heat a 10-inch ovenproof skillet, preferably cast iron, over medium heat. Add the chard mixture and pour the remaining 3 tablespoons of olive oil around the edges. Pour the egg mixture into the skillet—the pan will be very full. Cook, pulling the edges of the cooked eggs toward the center with a spatula, so that the loose, uncooked eggs are exposed to the heat. Once the edges are set, scatter the cheese over the top and place the skillet in the oven.

Bake until the frittata is set and the cheese is nicely melted, 5 to 7 minutes. The center should not be wobbly, and will puff up a bit. Run a knife around the edge of the skillet to loosen the fritatta. Place a large plate on top of the skillet and flip it over. The frittata should come out easily. Place another plate on top, flip the plates over, so that the browned portion is on top. Cut into bite-sized squares and serve at once or at room temperature.

(If you make the frittata ahead of time and refrigerate it, bring it to room temperature before cutting and serving.)

SERVES 8

Roasted Asparagus with Aioli

For the simplest, quickest, and tastiest results, roast asparagus on a baking sheet. This is a great alternative to the traditional European approach of bundling bunches in string and steaming or boiling them in salted water. The asparagus spears can be eaten with the fingers and dipped into the Aioli.

Break off the ends of the asparagus spears where they give and discard. Peel off the tough outer flesh of the lower part of fat asparagus spears so that the whole stalk is edible. With thin spears, just peel the bottom part. Peeling makes for faster cooking and an elegant smoother taste.

Preheat oven to 400°F.

Separate the spears into fat and thin piles. Arrange them on baking sheets in one layer, so that it will be easy to remove the thin ones first, as they get done.

Drizzle with the olive oil, season with salt and pepper, and roast for 10 minutes (7 minutes for thin spears), or until the ends can be easily pierced with a knife. Transfer the asparagus to a serving platter, tips going in one direction. Repeat the process with the remaining asparagus. Serve with the Aioli.

SERVES 6 TO 8

2 pounds asparagus

⅓ cup extra-virgin olive oil

Salt and freshly ground black pepper

Aioli (page 53)

Cecelia Chiang's Minced Chicken in Lettuce Cups (Chao Ji Song)

10 dried black Chinese mushrooms

3 tablespoons peanut oil

2 tablespoons minced ginger

2 cloves garlic, minced

2 pounds ground chicken
(¼ pound per person)

3 tablespoons Chinese rice wine

3 tablespoons dark mushroom
soy sauce

3 tablespoons Japanese soy sauce

¼ cup oyster sauce

Freshly ground white pepper

4 scallions, white part only,
trimmed and minced

⅓ cup pine nuts, roasted

6 to 10 iceberg lettuce leaves, cut
into manageable cups for holding
in the hand

This dish, based on the famous Cantonese recipe for squab, was one of the most memorable from Cecelia Chiang's Mandarin restaurant in Ghirardelli Square. The lettuce cups make for manageable eating at a stand-up party and add zing to a buffet. If you cannot find some of the ingredients at your grocery store, go to an Asian market for the mushrooms, Chinese rice wine, and dark mushroom soy sauce (or substitute button mushrooms, sherry, and conventional soy sauce).

Soak the mushrooms in a bowl of hot water until soft, about an hour. Remove from the soaking water and trim off the stems. Discard the water and stems. Finely chop the mushroom caps and set aside.

In a wok or large nonstick skillet, heat the oil over high heat. Add the ginger and garlic and stir-fry until fragrant, about 10 seconds. Add the chicken and stir-fry, breaking the meat up with a metal spatula, until it is no longer raw, about 2 minutes. Add the rice wine, soy sauces, oyster sauce, white pepper, and reserved mushrooms, and stir-fry for 2 minutes longer. Remove from the heat and add the scallions and pine nuts.

Spoon the chicken mixture into the lettuce cups on a large platter. Serve hot.

SERVES 6 TO 8

DOUBLE-DECKER CAVIAR CAKE

Shown on page 158

4 ounces salmon eggs, or other caviar

One 8-ounce package cream cheese

2 chives or 1 green onion, very finely chopped

This is so easy that it was the first hors' d'oeuvre I helped my mother make when I was ten. The salmon eggs are dazzling when they catch a bit of candlelight, but depending upon your budget, use whatever type of caviar you choose.

Divide the cream cheese into two balls. Flatten them with the palms of your hands. Place one on a plate and spread with ⅓ of the salmon eggs. Carefully place the second flattened layer of cream cheese on top of the salmon eggs. Spread the remaining salmon eggs on the sides of the "cake." Scatter the chives on top and serve with crackers or Pita Crisps (page 82).

SERVES 6 TO 8

FLOURLESS CHOCOLATE NEST CAKE

FOR THE CAKE

8 ounces good-quality dark chocolate

8 tablespoons (1 stick) unsalted butter, softened

6 large eggs: 2 whole; 4 separated

½ cup plus ⅓ cup sugar

1 teaspoon vanilla extract

Although this is a cocktail party menu, people often linger longer than we think and I like to have something sweet to offer when they do. Anyone can make this alluring cake—it falls, it cracks, and it is still good. The cake was inspired by a Nigella Lawson recipe in the New York Times.

If your party is around Easter, decorate it with chocolate malt eggs in speckled pale spring colors. It also works as a Passover dessert because it has no flour. If your party is around Valentine's Day, scatter cinnamon hearts in the frosting. Or use your imagination and come up with toppings of your own—chocolate rock candies, candied violets, candied rose petals. Just make sure that they are not too hard when you bite into them.

Preheat the oven to 350°F.

Butter the sides and bottom of a 9-inch springform cake pan.

TO MAKE THE CAKE

In a small bowl, melt the chocolate and butter in a microwave for 1 minute, or place in a small, heavy saucepan over medium-low heat. Let the mixture cool in the refrigerator or at room temperature. Set aside.

In a large bowl, beat 4 egg whites until foamy. Gradually add the ½ cup sugar. Continue beating until the whites are glossy and form moderately stiff peaks. Set aside.

In a medium bowl, whisk the 2 whole eggs and 4 egg yolks with the ⅓ cup sugar and vanilla until creamy. Fold the chocolate mixture into it.

Using a rubber spatula, working from bottom to top, gently fold one third of the egg whites into the chocolate mixture. When incorporated, fold in another third of the whites and gently combine again. Repeat with the remaining egg whites. You should not be able to see any egg white peeking through.

Pour the batter into the prepared pan. Bake in the top third of the oven for 35 to 40 minutes. The cake will rise, the sides will crack slightly, and, when done, the center will no longer be shaky.

Cool the cake completely on a wire rack. Don't worry, the center caves in a bit and the sides crack to form a nest. Remove the cake from the springform and from the bottom of the pan, and place it on a cake plate. (The cake can be made up to this point a day ahead of time and wrapped loosely in plastic wrap.)

TO MAKE THE FROSTING

Just before serving, whip together the frosting ingredients until it becomes glossy but not overly stiff. With a rubber spatula, drop the frosting in the middle of the cake and spread it out to the edges.

Scatter the decorations on top.

SERVES 6 TO 8

FOR THE FROSTING

1 cup heavy whipping cream

1 teaspoon vanilla extract

¼ cup sweetened cocoa powder such as Scharffen Berger or another excellent quality hot chocolate powder

FOR DECORATION

Approximately 1 cup of chocolate malted Easter egg candies
OR
½ cup cinnamon hearts, candied violets or rose petals, or rock candies

A One-Dish
Duck Dinner

Tuna Tapenade on Toast

. . . . .

Persimmon and Pomegranate Salad

. . . . .

Crispy Duck Legs with
Herbs and Flageolet Beans

. . . . .

Floating Island Pudding

uying duck is one of the great pleasures of living in France, and there is excellent duck available in the States as well (see Sources, page 217). Since I've lived in France, I've discovered that cooking duck is surprisingly easy. I used to be a breast girl, but now I prefer the flavor and tenderness of slow-cooked legs.

A platter of succulent, crisply browned duck legs resting on tender, baked flageolet beans is one of the easiest and most satisfying meals I prepare during the winter months. The savory, assertive flavors of the tuna tapenade hors d'oeuvre set up a play of flavorful contrasts with the sweet and bitter persimmon salad and the mellow beans and herb-crisped duck. The dessert—my favorite—floating island pudding always makes guests feel well cared for and a little nostalgic. It is a classic French dessert with soft meringues floating in a pool of crème anglaise with a drizzle of caramel over the top.

There is a wine store just downstairs from my apartment. The sellers love to eat, and are always helpful but a little amused by me, the American who cooks so much. The first time I made this dish I asked for a suggestion of what to serve with duck, and to my complete delight the seller asked, "Leg or breast?" I ended up with a great choice—for legs, a hearty Beaujolais Moulin a Vent. But they said a robust Côtes du Rhône would do just as well.

PARTY PLAN

THE DAY BEFORE

- Soak the beans
- Salt the duck legs

DAY OF THE PARTY

- Make the tapenade
- Make toasts
- Remove seeds from pomegranate
- Cook the beans
- Brown and bake the duck legs
- Make the dessert
- Make the salad dressing

DECORATING IDEAS

Place small vases filled with multicolored freesias around a cluster of white, unscented votive candles.

Tuna Tapenade on Toast

One 6 ½-ounce can imported tuna, packed in oil

2 teaspoons thyme leaves, minced

2 green onions, minced (white part mostly)

12 imported green olives, pitted, chopped

3 tablespoons capers, rinsed, drained

1 tablespoon lemon juice

Zest of 1 lemon

¼ cup extra-virgin olive oil

Freshly ground black pepper

Toasted slices of a good country loaf

This full-flavored spread is a twist on the traditional French tapenade of pureed olives. Using good imported tuna mixed with herbs, green onions, and lemon, it makes a substantial hors d'oeuvre.

Place all the ingredients in the bowl of a food processor and pulse to combine (save a little of the lemon zest for topping). The mixture should be chunky. Refrigerate until ready to use. Float a little olive oil on top if you are going to store it for more than a day, or if the tapenade needs more moisture and richness.

To serve, spread the tapenade on toasts and grate a little lemon zest on top.

SERVES 4 TO 6

Pitting Olives

Lay the olives on a clean work surface. With the flat side of a heavy knife, whack each olive to split it open. Ease the pit out with your fingers.

PERSIMMON AND POMEGRANATE SALAD

It is the French custom to serve a composed salad such as this for a first course, and then have a simple green salad as a sort of palate cleanser after the meal, before dessert. Sweet persimmons go beautifully with duck and provide a splash of color to a winter table. Their sugariness is tempered with a balsamic vinaigrette and the slightly sour pomegranate seeds. Short, squat Fuyu persimmons, eaten when crisp, are the ones to use here. The acorn-shaped Hachiya must ripen to a gelatinous softness to be edible and are the ones usually used for baking.

TO MAKE THE DRESSING

Place the shallot in a small bowl, sprinkle with salt and pepper to taste, and add the vinegars. Allow the shallot to macerate for a few minutes, then whisk in the olive oil.

TO PREPARE THE SALAD

Place the persimmons in a small bowl. Place the arugula and radicchio leaves in medium bowl. Divide the dressing between the persimmon slices and the greens and toss both mixtures.

Arrange the greens on a platter and scatter the persimmons over the top, tucking a few in under the leaves so the salad is not top-heavy. Then sprinkle the pomegranate seeds on top.

FOR THE DRESSING

1 large shallot, minced

1 tablespoon balsamic vinegar

2 tablespoons red wine vinegar

Salt and freshly ground black pepper

½ cup extra-virgin olive oil

FOR THE SALAD

2 small Fuyu persimmons (about 3 ounces each), peeled, halved, and thinly sliced

4 cups small arugula leaves, washed

2 cups radicchio leaves

1 small pomegranate (about 3 ounces), seeds removed and membrane discarded (½ cup seeds)

CRISPY DUCK LEGS WITH
HERBS AND FLAGEOLET BEANS

FOR THE BEANS

¼ cup extra-virgin olive oil

2 slices bacon, diced

8 shallots, thinly sliced

1 pound flageolet beans, soaked
overnight, and drained

2 sprigs fresh thyme, or
½ teaspoon dried thyme

1 bay leaf

1 cup chicken stock

1 bunch Swiss chard, washed,
tough stems removed

Salt and freshly ground
black pepper

FOR THE DUCK

6 to 8 duck legs and thighs

Salt and freshly ground
black pepper

2 sprigs fresh rosemary, chopped,
or ½ teaspoon of dried rosemary,
extra sprigs for finishing the dish

6 to 8 sprigs fresh thyme, chopped
or 1 tablespoon dried thyme

Since so many restaurants serve duck breasts, there are usually lots of duck legs left over at my butcher in San Francisco. This is a festive party dish. Prepare the beans in advance and serve the duck legs on top. Look for pale green and white flageolets or use dried great northern, or other small white beans. Soak the beans overnight, or for at least 12 hours.

TO PREPARE THE BEANS

Preheat the oven to 375°F.

Heat the olive oil in a large enameled or cast-iron casserole over medium heat. Add the bacon, and cook until it begins to crisp. Add the shallots and cook until they soften, about 2 minutes. Add the beans, thyme, and bay leaf, and stir to combine. Add the chicken stock and enough water to cover the beans. Cover the beans with parchment paper, cut to the size of the top of the casserole.

Bake the beans for 2½ to 3 hours, stirring occasionally (remove parchment each time). Taste to make sure beans are tender. Meanwhile, blanch the chard for 3 minutes in a pot of salted boiling water. Drain. Stir the chard into the beans. If there is too much liquid for serving, remove the excess with a baster. Season with salt and pepper to taste.

TO PREPARE THE DUCK LEGS

When you get the duck legs home, season them generously with salt and pepper and some of the chopped herbs before refrigerating them.

Preheat the oven to 350°F.

Heat a large, nonstick skillet over medium-high heat. Add the duck legs, skin side down, and brown for 3 to 5 minutes. Turn and brown them for another 3 to 5 minutes. Keep pouring off the fat so that it does not burn.

When the legs are browned, transfer to an ovenproof skillet, skin side down. Sprinkle on the herbs, and cook until the meat is falling off the bone, 1 hour and 15 minutes. Pour off excess fat if it begins to brown and smoke.

Serve the duck on top of the beans in a shallow serving dish, pour a little of the fat on top and lay a sprig or two of rosemary on top for serving.

SERVES 6

FLOATING ISLAND PUDDING

FOR THE CRÈME ANGLAISE

6 large egg yolks, beaten

½ cup sugar

2 cups whole milk

3-inch length of vanilla bean, split, or 2 teaspoons vanilla extract

FOR THE MERINGUE

4 large egg whites, at room temperature

Pinch of salt

Pinch of cream of tartar

2 tablespoons sugar

FOR THE CARAMEL

½ cup sugar

1 tablespoon water

I was having lunch with a friend at a little Parisian restaurant, and we each chose a floating island pudding for dessert. But before it arrived, my friend, Richard Overstreet, offered a treatise on floating islands. He theorized that sometimes the dessert was about the island (the soft meringues) and other times it was about the sea of liquid (the crème anglaise) that surrounds the island. He speculated that in comparison to the island, there is either an ocean, a lake, a pond, or a puddle. I love meringues, so to me, this dessert is really all about the islands, with just a bit of a pond for them to float in. Richard knows the woman who makes the best floating islands in all of Paris, so he arranged for a cooking session with Inez Casalderry to get the recipe and technique—and here it is.

This dessert can be made ahead of time and refrigerated until ready to serve. And though there are three steps, they are all undemanding.

TO MAKE THE CRÈME ANGLAISE

In a medium-sized bowl, whisk the yolks and the sugar.

Place the milk and the vanilla bean in a medium-sized saucepan and cook over medium heat until it just begins to boil. Remove from the heat and allow the vanilla bean to steep for a few minutes, and then remove and discard it.

Add a little of the hot milk to the egg mixture, and whisk to combine. Pour that mixture into the rest of the hot milk and combine again. Simmer over low heat until the custard thickens to the consistency of heavy cream, stirring constantly. It is the proper consistency when you dip a spoon into it, pull it out, then run your finger down the bowl of the spoon, if a line forms, it is done. Or use an instant-read thermometer; the sauce is done when it registers 170°F. (But watch carefully, if it curdles, you will have to start over.)

Pour the sauce through a fine-meshed sieve into a 1-quart round or oval serving dish with a good lip, stir it occasionally as it cools. Set aside.

TO MAKE THE MERINGUE

In the bowl of a stand mixer or with a handheld mixer in a bowl, beat together the egg whites, salt, cream of tartar, and sugar until glossy peaks form.

Add a quart or 2 of water to a large skillet and bring it to a simmer. Spread out a clean kitchen towel next to the stove on a flat work surface.

Form the egg whites with a tablespoon into dollops (or islands) that are

tablespoon size or larger. Float the dollops in the barely simmering water. Poach for no more than 5 seconds per side, turning them gently with a slotted spoon. Remove with the slotted spoon, allowing some of the poaching water to drip off before placing them on the towel. Repeat until all the egg white mixture is used.

Using a slotted spoon, transfer the meringues onto the crème anglaise in the serving dish.

NOTE: I like to really stuff the meringues on. If you prefer to have more of the sauce visible, use fewer islands. But plan on at least 1 or 2 per person.

TO MAKE THE CARAMEL

In a small, heavy saucepan combine the sugar and water over low heat. Swirl the pan over the heat for 5 to 7 minutes, until the syrup becomes a deep amber color. Then immediately use a spoon to drizzle the caramel over the islands in a back and forth motion. Refrigerate the whole dish until ready to serve.

SERVES 6

A SUPPER
FOR CHILLY NIGHTS

Basket of Crisp Vegetables

(PAGE 122)

· · · · ·

Tartiflette

· · · · ·

Winter Greens with
Sherry Vinaigrette and Pine Nuts

· · · · ·

Orange Carpaccio

The first chill of winter always makes me want to invite friends over, light a fire, and make this peasant meal centered around the oozing cheese dish from the Haute-Savoie region of France called *tartiflette*. It's a baked affair, hearty with wintery ingredients, that requires nothing more for accompaniment than a bowl of bitter greens tossed with a sherry vinaigrette, and the delightfully clean and cheerful orange carpaccio. I like to balance the rich main course with the flash of acidity from the salad and tartness of the citrus dessert.

I love to serve *tartiflette* to my American friends because it is something most of them haven't had, and when I serve this dish in France, my guests are often surprised that an Amerian would know about it. It is rich, with melted cheese, potatoes, and bacon, and comes to the table in the dish in which it was baked—always causing a stir.

I recommend serving a basket of chilled raw vegetables or some good imported olives with drinks before dinner. You want to save room for the *tartiflette*.

PARTY PLAN

THE DAY BEFORE

- Prepare the dessert

DAY OF THE PARTY

- Slice and chill raw vegetables
- Prepare the potatoes
- Cook the bacon and the onions
- Wash the greens
- Make the vinaigrette

DECORATING IDEAS

Buy eight to ten ivory-colored candles (unscented) of different widths and heights. Put them on a copper or silver tray and place them in the center of the table. They produce a warm, flickering glow.

TARTIFLETTE

4 pounds Yukon gold potatoes, peeled and cut into 1-inch dice

1 bay leaf

¾ bottle dry white wine

Salt and freshly ground black pepper

2 large onions, cut into 1-inch dice

⅓ pound thick-cut bacon, cut into 1-inch dice

1 whole Reblochon or Pont l'Eveque cheese, cut in half horizontally

From my first bite of tartiflette I knew it was destined to become part of my repertoire. The concept is definitely simple, and the dish can be prepared in advance. Just slice open a strong, runny cheese such as Reblochon, Pont l'Eveque, Muenster, or Epoisses, stuff it with potatoes cooked with bacon and onions, replace the top of the cheese, and bake until molten. It can be warmed once the guests arrive.

Preheat the oven to 425°F.

Place the potatoes in a large roasting pan along with the bay leaf and wine. If the wine does not completely cover the potatoes, add a little water. Season generously with salt and pepper. Bake for 15 to 20 minutes, or until the potatoes are tender.

Meanwhile, place the bacon in a large skillet over medium-high heat. Cook for about 7 minutes or until the bits begin to get brown and crispy. Add the onions and cook until they become translucent, about 3 minutes.

Remove the potatoes from the oven. Using a slotted spoon, transfer potatoes to the skillet with the bacon and onions. Leave about ½ cup of the liquid in the roasting pan, pour the rest of the liquid into a bowl, and set aside. Stir the potatoes into the bacon and onion mixture and taste for seasoning.

If there is a hard tough rind on the cheese, slice most of it off with a sharp knife and discard. Place one half of the cheese on the bottom of a round or oval gratin-style baking dish. Pour the potato mixture over and around the cheese. Place the top half of the cheese on the potato mixture. If the mixture seems a little dry, add some of the reserved wine and/or a little water. (If you are making this dish in advance, prepare it to this point and refrigerate. Bring to room temperature, then bake it until the potatoes are hot, about 20 minutes.)

Bake for 15 minutes, or until the potatoes are hot and the cheese is oozing and bubbling. Serve from the baking dish at the table.

SERVES 6 TO 8

WINTER GREENS WITH SHERRY VINAIGRETTE AND PINE NUTS

FOR THE DRESSING

1 large shallot minced

Pinch of sea salt

3 tablespoons sherry vinegar

½ cup extra-virgin olive oil

⅓ cup toasted pine nuts

6 cups bitter greens, washed and chilled

Fill a salad bowl with assorted bitter winter greens, such as escarole, endive, radicchio, and dandelion greens. A bottle of good sherry vinegar is a great pantry item—it brings a sparkle to soups such as gazpacho and offers a change from red wine vinegar in vinaigrettes.

Place the shallot in a small bowl with the salt and the vinegar, and allow the shallot to macerate for a few minutes. Whisk in the olive oil. Toss the dressing with the greens and sprinkle the nuts on top.

SERVES 6

ORANGE CARPACCIO

12 oranges

5 tablespoons sugar

1 vanilla bean, split

1 cinnamon stick

2 cloves

1 star anise

A handful of red currants, pomegranate seeds, or raspberries

I had been delighted by this dessert of spiced oranges in zesty sauce many times at dinner parties in Paris and I finally I got up the nerve to ask for the recipe. The cook assumed I would understand how to make it with a simple description. When my attempts failed, I planned a cooking session to watch her, step by step. Now this is one of the highlights of my winter dessert collection. With its gentle sweetness and acidity, it is ideal to serve when you have prepared something rich, such as tartiflette, roast duck, or beef stew. Plan on about 1½ oranges per person. This dessert improves with age so it is a good idea to make it a day ahead of time or the morning of your dinner.

Use a 6-holed zesting device to remove the zest from the oranges into long, thin strips. Bring 1 cup of water to a boil in a small saucepan. Add the orange zest and blanch for about 3 minutes. Transfer the strands with a slotted spoon to a small strainer. Rinse with cold water and separate and drain on a towel.

In the same saucepan, combine the sugar with 1 cup of water, stir well, and bring to a simmer. Scrape out the interior of the vanilla bean into the saucepan. Add the cinnamon stick, cloves, and star anise and continue to simmer for about 10 minutes until the sauce reduces by about a third. It will have thickened slightly. Add the orange zest to the sauce, remove from the heat, and set aside.

Cut off the tips of the oranges so they stand upright steadily. Using careful, sculpting slices, remove the pith and remaining peel of the oranges with a very sharp knife. Cut the oranges into round slices about ¼ inch thick. Remove any stray pits.

Place the orange slices in a serving bowl, layering them with the sauce so that the zest is distributed evenly throughout. Top with the red currants and refrigerate. Serve chilled. Keeps in refrigerator for 3 days, well covered.

SERVES 8 TO 10

In Praise of Braising

Scallop Petals with Mâche

. . . .

Braised Lamb Shanks with
White Beans Swirled with Greens

Mint Sauce

. . . .

Apple Galette with Calvados

Braising is a dinner party host's best friend, and it is an easy technique to master. The idea is that once the ingredient is browned, it basically cooks in its own juices and a liquid (such as wine), in the oven or on top of the stove. The result is a tender, deep-flavored dish, great for a party. I made these braised lamb shanks for the parties that I would have whenever my vegetarian boyfriend went away. My meat-loving friends anticipated his departure with unstinting enthusiasm, knowing they were hours away from what we rebelliously called "a meat party." When they called to determine the plans, they'd find it amusing that I'd often be home from dropping him off at the airport by 7:00 AM and already browning my lamb shanks.

For this one-dish meal, the white beans are swirled with the greens and the lamb shanks are served on top to create a multilayered, dense, and extremely satisfying party dish that is a feast for the eyes as well. A drizzle of fresh mint sauce sparks all of the components. When serving a meaty and robust main course, I like to start with a delicate dish such as the petals of scallops, and end with a flaky apple galette.

PARTY PLAN

THE DAY BEFORE

- Soak the beans
- Wash the greens
- Make the galette dough

DAY OF THE PARTY

- Cook the beans
- Brown and then braise the lamb shanks
- Braise the greens
- Make the galette

LAST MINUTE

- Prepare the scallops
- Assemble the elements of the lamb dish, reheating each separately
- Gently reheat the galette
- Whip the cream

DECORATING IDEAS

Place bunches or small pots of narcissus in glass or silver vases around the room (but not on the table as their aroma is too intoxicating near the food).

Scallop Petals with Mâche

1 pound day-boat scallops, or other impeccably fresh sea scallops

2 heads mâche, about 3 handfuls

2 tablespoons fresh lemon juice

6 tablespoons extra-virgin olive oil, preferably a mild French Provençal variety

Salt and freshly ground black pepper

Shaving of black truffles (optional)

I was captivated by the name of this dish when I first had it in Paris. It's a light and appropriate beginning to such a rich meal. In winter, it can be served with slices of black truffle, should you find them. In order to create the petal look, the scallops must be chilled, then sliced very, very thin. Mâche, or lamb's lettuce, is the best green to use, but small Bibb lettuces can be used if you can't find mâche.

Chill the scallops in the freezer for about 15 minutes. Remove them from the freezer and slice as thin as possible, about 6 to 8 slices per large scallop. Put them in a bowl, cover with plastic wrap, and set aside.

Wash and dry the mâche. Make a dressing by whisking together the lemon juice, olive oil, and salt and pepper to taste. Toss one half of it with the mâche in a small bowl.

Arrange the scallop slices on a large serving platter in one overlapping layer, like petals. Then pour the remaining dressing over the scallops. Season generously with salt and pepper. Scatter the truffles on top, if using. Place the mâche in one large bundle, almost as a garnish, but guests may help themselves to a few leaves. You may want to have this course on the table as your guests sit down.

SERVES 6

BRAISED LAMB SHANKS WITH WHITE BEANS SWIRLED WITH GREENS

FOR THE BEANS

1½ pounds dried white beans, about 3 cups

2 tablespoons extra-virgin olive oil

2 sprigs fresh sage

1 clove garlic, crushed with the back of a knife

1 Parmesan rind (optional)

Sea salt and freshly ground black pepper

FOR THE GREENS

4 to 6 cups greens (chard, escarole, Tuscan kale, or dandelion greens in any combination), washed, tough stems removed, and chopped

3 tablespoons extra-virgin olive oil

2 sprigs fresh sage, or 1 teaspoon dried sage, crumbled

1 clove garlic, crushed with the back of a knife

2 anchovy fillets

Sea salt and freshly ground black pepper

Because the flavors of braised dishes improve with a little time, this dish can be made a day in advance or at least a few hours before the party. You cannot go wrong with this dish; it always works and it is positively succulent. The lamb, beans, and greens are all cooked separately until very tender, then the greens are swirled into the beans and the whole meal is served in one dish with the shanks on top. The mint sauce adds another touch of green.

Start with the beans or work on them once they are soaked and the shanks are braising. Buy dried beans from a store with lots of turnover so you can find the freshest ones possible. At home, carefully pick over them to remove any pebbles. Large white beans, cannellini, or Great Northern beans can be used for this recipe. If you have a rind of Parmesan in your refrigerator, throw it into the beans as they cook; it adds a mysterious richness. Do not overstir the beans or they will break up and become too starchy.

TO COOK THE BEANS

Soak the beans in 2 quarts of cold water overnight or for at least a few hours. Drain well. In a large pot, heat the olive oil over medium heat. Add the sage and garlic, then beans, and 4 cups of water or enough water to cover the beans by 2 inches. Bring to a simmer and add the cheese rind.

Stir gently and continue to simmer until the beans are tender, about 1½ hours if the beans are fresh; up to 2½ hours if they are old. When done, drain off any excess liquid, (saving some for reheating the beans), season with salt and pepper to taste, and set aside.

TO PREPARE THE GREENS

Drop the greens into a large pot of salted boiling water and blanch for 3 minutes. Drain and press out the excess liquid. Heat the olive oil in the same pot over medium heat. Add the garlic and anchovies, stirring for a minute or two until the anchovies melt into the oil and the garlic is translucent. Add the greens and continue to cook, stirring occasionally, until they are tender, about 20 minutes. Set aside for up to 3 hours. Stir the greens into the pot of beans so that they swirl through the mixture.

TO PREPARE THE LAMB SHANKS

Preheat the oven to 400°F.

Season the lamb shanks generously with salt and pepper. Warm 2 tablespoons of the olive oil over medium-high heat in a heavy braising pan that will hold all of the shanks (or use two pans). Add the shanks and brown them on all sides, 10 to 15 minutes. Transfer the shanks to a large plate and set aside. Pour off the fat but keep the crispy bits at the bottom of the pan. Add the remaining olive oil to the pan along with the onion, garlic, and rosemary. Cook, stirring up the crispy bits on the bottom, until the onions become translucent, a few minutes. Return the shanks to the pan and pour the wine over them.

Place the pan, uncovered, in the oven and cook for about 40 minutes. Check to see if the wine has begun to evaporate, if so, add the chicken stock. Cover the pan and continue to cook for 1½ hours more, turning the shanks occasionally. You may need to add a little extra stock if the liquid level drops. When done, the meat should be very tender, almost falling off the bone. (The shanks can rest in their juices for a few hours at room temperature or they can be refrigerated for a day, brought back to room temperature and reheated, with a little extra water, if needed. Then proceed with the recipe.)

Transfer the shanks to a platter and discard the rosemary sprig, cover, and keep warm on top of the stove. Remove as much of the fat as possible from the pan juices and then pour the juices over the meat.

If made in advance, reheat the lamb shanks in their juices in a pan big enough to hold them on top of the stove. Swirl the greens into the beans and gently reheat on top of the stove.

TO ASSEMBLE THE DISH

Pour the bean mixture onto a large warm platter. Arrange the warm lamb shanks on top and dot them with a little mint sauce. Serve the remaining mint sauce on the side.

SERVES 6

FOR THE LAMB SHANKS

6 lamb shanks, 10 to 12 ounces each. Have your butcher trim the shank bone to remove the long ends.

Salt and freshly ground black pepper

⅓ cup extra-virgin olive oil

1 medium onion, sliced

8 cloves garlic, crushed with the back of a knife

1 sprig fresh rosemary

½ bottle dry white wine

½ cup chicken stock or water

Mint Sauce (page 186)

Mint Sauce

4 cups fresh mint, leaves and tender stems, washed

⅓ cup champagne vinegar or apple cider vinegar

3 tablespoons sugar

This bright, fresh accompaniment to lamb is one of the first recipes I learned to make as a girl. It should be made 1 hour before serving.

Place the mint, vinegar, and sugar in a food processor or blender. Process until the leaves are pureed with the other ingredients.

MAKES ABOUT 1 CUP

Apple Galette with Calvados

FOR THE PASTRY

2 cups all-purpose flour

1 cup (2 sticks) unsalted butter, very cold, cut into ½-inch cubes

1 large egg yolk (save the white for the filling)

1 tablespoon sugar

¼ teaspoon salt

¼ cup or more sparkling water, very cold

FOR THE FILLING

8 to 10 medium-sized apples, Galas, Fujis, or other substantial type

About 1 cup granulated sugar

1½ tablespoons dark brown sugar

2 tablespoons fresh lemon juice

Believe it or not, I made this winter dessert twelve times one season after learning the technique. One secret to the dough is butter, but using sparkling water, such as Perrier, is a secret French touch that insures flakiness. A galette is a good choice for parties because it can be made a few hours before serving and reheated slightly in the oven, if desired. Try it with pears, peaches, figs and berries at other times of the year.

I have adapted the recipe to the American kitchen, and I recommend that you make the dough by hand, not in the food processor. Double the pastry recipe and freeze half of it because you will want to make this dessert again and again.

TO MAKE THE PASTRY

In a large bowl, rub the flour, butter, egg yolk, sugar, and salt together with your fingers until it looks like coarse meal; it will take about 5 minutes The butter should not be completely mixed in, but still be visible in tiny pieces. Add the cold water in small amounts, just until the dough starts to hold together. Do not overwork the dough or it will make a tough crust.

Pat the dough into a ball and flatten it into a disk with smooth edges (pat away any cracks on the periphery or it will have cracks and holes when it is rolled out). Wrap the disk tightly in plastic wrap and refrigerate for at least an hour and up to two days before rolling out.

TO MAKE THE FILLING

Peel, core, and cut each apple into 8 to 10 pieces lengthwise, depending upon their size. In a large bowl, toss the apples very gently with enough of the granulated sugar to sweeten to your taste, then add the brown sugar, lemon, butter, Calvados, and flour. Set aside as you roll out the dough.

TO ASSEMBLE

Preheat the oven to 425°F.

On a floured work surface, roll the dough out to a large circle about 15 inches in diameter. Place the round on a nonstick sheet pan or one lined with parchment. Patch any holes. Mound the filling on the pastry, leaving a 3-inch border of dough around the edge. Pour any remaining liquid left from the filling over the top.

Fold the 3-inch border of dough in overlapping folds over the outer edge of the apple circle, being careful not to create any holes so the juice will not run out (if necessary, patch holes with pieces of dough as you go). The dough will overlap in places, which lends a rustic appearance. The center of the galette will be open. Brush the pastry border with the egg white mixed with a splash of water, then sprinkle with about 1 tablespoon of the granulated sugar.

Bake in the top half of the oven for 40 to 45 minutes or until the crust is browned and the apples are bubbling. Let cool slightly then serve with crème fraîche or sweetened whipped cream flavored with a little more Calvados.

SERVES 6

2 tablespoons unsalted butter, cut into small pieces

Splash of Calvados, optional

2 tablespoons all-purpose flour

1 large egg white

FOR THE TOPPING (OPTIONAL)

1 cup crème fraîche or 1 cup heavy whipping cream flavored with confectioners' sugar and a splash of Calvados

ANY EXCUSE FOR PORK

Cucumber Rounds with Smoked Trout
and Horseradish Cream

· · · · ·

Seed-and-Herb-Crusted Pork Tenderloin

· · · · ·

Roasted Radicchio with Gorgonzola

· · · · ·

Popovers

· · · · ·

Marsala Gelée

My butcher shop in Paris is about as close to a museum of meat as they come. It is a jewel of a store with an elaborate little cage for the cashier, marble everywhere, and a radiance from the attentively arranged counters. The meats are so handsomely selected and cut, they could convert a vegetarian on the spot. I walk through St. Germain, over the Seine past Notre Dame and down the narrow streets of Ile St. Louis to the butcher shop. A sighting of the handsome young butcher is sufficient to pull any woman (and some men), out of a dark mood. I have been on a pork kick, I tell him. I brought wild fennel seeds and pollen with me from California and want to use them to concoct an herby, spicy crust for the meat. So I ask for a few tenderloins of pork, which he wraps in white paper and ties with butcher string. He, like so many other purveyors, tells me exactly how to cook it and how long to let it rest once done.

This menu is meaty and earthy, so I like to start with a smoked trout and cucumber hors d'oeuvre. The pork tenderloins are rubbed with a crunchy seed-and-herb coating, then enlivened with a dash of balsamic vinegar. Yeasty popovers harmonize with the strong flavors of roasted radicchio and Gorgonzola. The meal ends on a boozy note with the Marsala gelée.

PARTY PLAN

THE DAY BEFORE

- Make the gelée

DAY OF THE PARTY

- Prepare ingredients for last-minute assembly of trout and cucumber
- Rub the tenderloins with salt, spices, and herbs
- Assemble the radicchio and gorgonzola in a baking dish
- Prepare the popover batter

DECORATING IDEAS

On a solid-colored cloth or on the surface of the dining table, run beautiful, unusual ribbons of different widths and types down the center to make a runner that drops off the edge of the table. The ribbons can be of uneven lengths and can be held in place with a tiny bit of tape on the back of each. Finish each ribbon with an inverted V or at an angle. Use napkins that match the colors of the ribbons. Flowers or fruit that complement the ribbons can be used as a centerpiece.

Cucumber Rounds with Smoked Trout and Horseradish Cream

1 English cucumber, peeled

¼ cup crème fraîche

1 tablespoon prepared horseradish

2 to 4 ounces smoked trout

Squeeze of lemon juice

2 chives, minced

Here's the perfect last-minute hors d'oeuvre when you want something light and straightforward. You can use any smoked fish you like instead of the trout—salmon, sablefish, tuna, or bluefish.

Slice the cucumbers into ¾-inch rounds and arrange on a platter. Mix the crème fraîche with the horseradish in a small bowl.

Flake the smoked fish and put a tablespoon or so on each cucumber round. Spoon a dab of the horseradish cream on top. Top with lemon juice and chives.

SERVES 6

Roasted Radicchio with Gorgonzola

6 heads radicchio, cut into quarters

Splash of extra-virgin olive oil

Splash of balsamic vinegar

Salt

Freshly ground black pepper

⅓ pound Gorgonzola or other good blue cheese that will melt, cut into pieces

Here is a superb recipe I learned from Reed Hearon, the San Francisco chef. I make it often because it is so good and so incredibly easy. The bitter radicchio and salty-sweet gorgonzola melt into one another as they roast. Don't worry if the leaves become a little tarnished, they still will taste great. This makes an excellent accompaniment to pork, or any roasted meat or poultry. Look for radicchio di Treviso, the elongated version of the more familiar tight round radicchio. If you can't find it, use the round version.

Preheat the oven to 400°F.

Pack the radicchio tightly into a medium-sized gratin dish, cut side up. Drizzle with olive oil and a few drops of balsamic. Season with salt and pepper to taste. Dot with the cheese and roast for 10 to 15 minutes, until the cheese melts and the radicchio is tender. Serve from the baking dish.

SERVES 6

Seed-and-Herb-Crusted Pork Tenderloin

Wild fennel grows around San Francisco in parks, backyards, and along the coast. In the late summer and early fall, the yellow flowers can be harvested for their pollen to be rubbed on pork or fish. When the flowers go to seed in the fall, harvest them for this pork dish. Here the seeds are mixed with crunchy sea salt, herbs, and spices to make a delightful rub that is slightly rough in texture and delicious—the perfect combination with the pork. You can use store-bought fennel seeds in place of the wild fennel seeds or pollen (see Sources, page 217).

Once you get the meat home, sprinkle it liberally with salt. Salt does wonders for "the other white meat" that has been bred to be so svelte that it has lost much of its flavor. Since there is little fat on pork tenderloins, they are beautifully suited to stovetop cooking, at a high temperature. A lower temperature would dry out the meat before it gets brown and cooked through, advises Steve Johnson, master pork cook and the inspiration for this recipe.

Season the tenderloins with salt. Using a mortar and pestle or a food processor, pound or pulse the fennel seeds, coriander seeds, pepper, herbs, ginger, and sea salt. Rub the tenderloins with this mixture. Refrigerate for at least an hour or up to a day.

Heat a heavy skillet over medium-high heat, add the olive oil, and swirl it around the pan. Add the tenderloins and cook for 12 to 15 minutes, turning so that all sides are browned nicely. Drizzle with a little olive oil once you turn them. A meat thermometer inserted into the thickest part should read 140° to 145°F. when done. (Remove the skinniest part of the tenderloin, as it gets done first. Then continue to cook the rest of the cut until done.)

Remove the tenderloins from the skillet and allow them to rest; they will cook a little more. Pour a few drops of balsamic over the pork. Slice the tenderloins into thin rounds, arrange them on a platter, and drizzle with more balsamic. Pass the bottle of balsamic with the platter.

SERVES 6

3 pork tenderloins, about 8 to 10 ounces each

Generous sprinkling of salt

1 tablespoon fennel seeds or fennel pollen

1 tablespoon coriander seeds

½ teaspoon freshly ground black pepper

1 tablespoon herbes de Provence or chopped fresh herbs such as rosemary, oregano, or thyme

½ teaspoon ground ginger

2 teaspoons salt

1 tablespoon olive oil, plus more for drizzling

Aged balsamic vinegar

POPOVERS

5 tablespoons unsalted butter, melted, plus 2 tablespoons for greasing pan

1½ cups all-purpose flour

1½ cups whole milk

1 teaspoon salt

3 large eggs

Popovers are a treat for breakfast, lunch, or dinner—an old-fashioned surprise. For best results, try to find popover pans where the metal cups are connected by a little bar. Alternatively, use individual Pyrex cups set on a baking sheet or a cast iron muffin pan (¾-cup size). A baking tip: If you peek at the popovers before 30 minutes, they may appear to be done, but the center will be doughy and heavy if you take them out too early.

Popover Memories

From my car radio recently, I heard the voice of a woman rhapsodizing over popovers of all things. And as I pushed my way through the traffic, I began to rhapsodize, too. The mere idea of making popovers brought back the sweetest memories of my father, the person I most loved being with in the kitchen. It was the only time I had him to myself. Since we both rose early, he kept me out of mischief by cooking with me. Our repertoire was small—it included only popovers. He listened to wrestling matches with my brother and drank martinis with my mother, but with me it was only popovers.

We experimented with recipes and with pans, deciding, after much deliberation, that a heavy iron muffin pan placed in a hot oven to warm up as the oven preheated was the best route to take. It was our science project, and no matter what my mother, the real cook of the family, said, we knew we had a winner on our hands. She was always after us to add cheese or mushrooms. Nancy Knickerbocker was a demanding perfectionist in the kitchen. I will have to admit that my love of cooking is due largely to her influence, but that didn't mean it was fun to be in the kitchen with her. There was one way to do things, and she had little tolerance for any deviation.

So my father and I had to get into the kitchen early enough to pull off our culinary pursuit, uncensored. We worked as she slept. Our mission never varied, it always involved the same recipe. And our popovers popped high, up over the sides of the black pan, without my mother's input. The popover's interior was airy and buttery. And I, lover of everything crispy and crunchy, ate only the tops. It was allowed; they were mine. My father ate them with Dundee Marmalade and a cup of strong tea. I ate mine with salted butter. Since popovers need to be eaten as soon as they come out of the oven, my father and I would eat the lot if my brother and mother didn't get up in time

If I could go back for one hour with my father, who died 20 years ago, it would be on a Saturday morning in the kitchen, with that sweet, doughy smell swirling around us.

Preheat the oven to 425°F. Remove the top rack from the oven; the popovers will be baked on the lower rack.

Grease each cup of the popover pan generously. (If using iron muffin pans, place them in the oven to preheat and butter them carefully once hot.)

Using a rotary beater or a whisk, beat all of the ingredients together until smooth. Using a ladle, fill the prepared cups halfway full with batter.

Bake in the bottom third of the oven for about 30 minutes, or until the popovers are golden and light. Serve at once; they fall quickly.

MAKES 6

Marsala Gelée

2 envelopes unflavored powdered gelatin

½ cup cold water

1 cup boiling water

¾ cup sugar

1⅔ cups Marsala or sherry

⅓ cup fresh lemon juice

1 cup heavy whipping cream beaten to soft peaks with a little sugar, optional

When we had this dessert growing up in San Francisco, we called it wine Jell-O; I always felt a little buzz from it. When I served it in Paris, my French guests got a kick out of it because they think American Jell-O is such an amusing concept. But they loved this sophisticated version and suggested the name change to Marsala gelée. If you want to calm the kick in this dessert, heat the Marsala for a few minutes first; the flavor will remain but the alcohol will be tempered. Be sure to make this the night before or at least 7 hours ahead, as it needs to jell.

In a large heatproof bowl, sprinkle the gelatin over the cold water and let it stand until softened, about 5 minutes. Add the boiling water and sugar and stir until completely dissolved. Stir in the Marsala and lemon juice and let cool to room temperature.

Transfer to a serving bowl and refrigerate until firm, at least 7 hours or preferably overnight. Spoon into dessert bowls, top each serving with a dollop of sweetened whipped cream, and serve.

SERVES 6

The Nancy Knickerbocker Kick

Recently I found my mother's white metal recipe box, hand-painted by my father with blue bachelor buttons, his favorite flower. That rusty old box had been missing for years, and when I opened it, I felt shivers of nostalgia as I looked at Nancy Knickerbocker's scrawl on the curling brown cards.

My mother kept our refrigerator stocked with exotic foods by 1950s standards—jars of capers, a crock of confit, and more often than not, a peculiar bowl of wobbly amber-colored gelatin. This concoction was indented with little spoon marks from my mother's constant nibbling. Made with sweet wine, it delivered a gloved punch that soothed her nerves. When she paid bills in the afternoon or tended to other household chores that seemed demanding to her, she felt perfectly deserving of a fortifying bite of that wine-laced dessert. As you will notice throughout this book, I include a few other recipes of hers, always cooked with some sort of liquor. While making Welsh rarebit, bourbon balls, or coq au vin, she'd gleefully proclaim "a little for the pot and a little for me."

As I sat at my kitchen table reading the recipes, separated with out-of-date dividers that read canapés, casseroles, and chafing dish, I was surprised to find that some were still worth making—Portuguese bean soup, Welsh rarebit, and that Marsala gelée, which we called wine Jell-O. I decided to test it on two of my favorite chefs, Alice Waters of Chez Panisse and Scott Warner of Don Giovanni in Napa. I invited them over for a meal that included bottarga, salty, air-dried fish roe that I had just smuggled home from a trip to Tunisia. I planned to shave it over a simple pasta and I needed a light, clean, clear dessert to follow. Wine gelée it was. I made one boozy batch and another with cooked Marsala for those who didn't want the Nancy Knickerbocker kick.

A few days later I got an email from the Chez Panisse kitchen requesting the recipe for a dinner at the restaurant. All her life, my mother read cookbooks and was fascinated with every aspect of cooking. She would have been so proud to know the legacy of her recipe, some 25 years after her death.

TRIO OF LAST-MINUTE SUPPERS

French Onion Soup with Gruyère Cheese Toasts

· · · · ·

Welsh Rarebit of Artisanal Cheddar and Guinness Stout

· · · · ·

Baked Asparagus with Poached Eggs and Fontina Cheese

· · · · ·

Classic Spinach Salad

· · · · ·

Bowl of Seasonal Fresh Fruit

You have been on a long drive, you have gone to the movies with friends, or it's Sunday evening and you do not feel like making a production over supper. Here are three swift, substantial ideas for delicious, low-key simple soirées. All three dishes feature a variation of melted cheese, which always provides a soothing effect on the palate and soul. Depending upon the season, most of the ingredients would or could be on hand for last-minute preparation.

The onion soup is the classic, cheese encrusted, brothy fare that was served at Les Halles, the bustling old Parisian market. It was the thing to have after a festive evening, just before calling it a night. This version is a little different in that the cheese gets melted on the toast separately and then placed on top of the soup, making the process easier and the end result less goopy.

Welsh rarebit takes on new life with the flavor of sharp, aged cheddar melted with the bitter caramel flavor of the Irish stout.

There is nothing like a poached egg breaking over roasted stalks of asparagus, both mingling with the grassy, nutlike flavor of melting Fontina.

With any of the three recipes, serve the spinach salad, a warm loaf of crusty bread, and a bowl of fresh fruit—sliced apples would be just the thing to go with the Welsh rarebit for dessert.

PARTY PLAN

The French onion soup can be made ahead of time and reheated at the last minute. The Welsh rarebit requires last-minute preparation, but it doesn't take long to make, and is so satisfying and easy. The asparagus literally takes just minutes to make. If you were coming home to prepare it, the asparagus could be arranged in the baking dish, the cheese grated, and the eggs would just need to be cracked on top and the dish baked.

DECORATING IDEAS

While these are last-minute suppers, bring out good glasses, linen, and plates to make up for their intrinsic simplicity.

French Onion Soup with Gruyère Cheese Toasts

2 tablespoons unsalted butter

2 tablespoons extra-virgin olive oil

3 pounds yellow onions, cut into ¼-inch slices

2 cloves garlic, chopped

Freshly ground black pepper

2 tablespoons all-purpose flour

1 tablespoon Dijon mustard

3 cups dry white wine, or dry red wine

2 bay leaves

6 cups chicken stock, preferably homemade

¾ pound Gruyère or other Swiss-type cheese, grated

Six 1-inch slices of rustic country bread, toasted and buttered

Salt

This is the onion soup of onion soups. I seek out this deep rich soup in restaurants when I am in Paris, usually without much luck unless I go to a tourist restaurant. So when I arrive, I make my own. This recipe comes from Christopher Hirsheimer, the photographer for this book and a great cook.

In a large, heavy pot melt the butter in the olive oil over medium-high heat. Add the onions and garlic and reduce the heat to medium. Cook, stirring continuously, for about 20 minutes or until the onions are nice and brown. Season with pepper.

Add the flour, stirring it into the mixture so it cooks for a minute or two. Add the mustard and stir to incorporate.

Add the wine and the bay leaves and cook for about 5 minutes. Add the stock a little at the time, and simmer very slowly for at least 30 minutes. If the stock is evaporating too quickly, or if you have an extra guest at the last moment, add a cup or two of extra stock or water.

Just before serving, preheat the oven to broil. Mound about two-thirds of the cheese on the toast slices and place them on a baking sheet. Broil, watching very carefully, until the cheese is melted and lightly browned.

Ladle the soup into warm soup bowls, add a tablespoon of cheese to each bowl for extra richness, and then float the cheese toast on top.

SERVES 4 TO 6

Tips for the Best Onion Soup

- Do not salt the onions while they are browning; salt causes the onions to sweat water and they will not brown as nicely.

- Make ahead: The soup and the broiled cheesy toasts can be made ahead of time and warmed and assembled at the last minute. Perfect for a late-night supper.

Welsh Rarebit of Artisanal Cheddar and Guinness Stout

1 pound aged (2 to 4 years) cheddar (such as a Cheshire cheese with a good crumb) grated

½ cup Guinness stout

1 teaspoon English dry mustard mixed with a little water

Dash of cayenne pepper

1 egg yolk, beaten (optional)

4 slices crusty country loaf, toasted and buttered
OR
1 head of steamed cauliflower, left whole

We had Welsh rarebit so often when I was growing up that I really couldn't face it again for years until I had a version for lunch recently at one of my favorite restaurants, St. John's, in the meatpacking area of London. One of the reasons many of us are not particularly fond of this dish is because, during my childhood at least, it was served on bland whole wheat toast using tasteless cheddar cheese. It needs an exceptionally good bread, toasted; it is also beautiful and delicious poured on a steamed head of cauliflower. The trick I learned at St. John's Restaurant is to make it with Guinness stout.

Place a double boiler over high heat until the water in the bottom half is boiling. Add the cheese to the top part of the double boiler, a little at a time, stirring constantly. Add 1 or 2 tablespoons of the stout. Once the cheese begins to melt reduce the heat to medium-low. As it begins to thicken, add the rest of the stout and stir with a wooden spoon.

Continue to stir while you add the mustard and the cayenne. Add the egg and whisk the mixture well. Continue to stir until the mixture becomes smooth and slightly thickened.

To serve, you can either pour the Welsh rarebit over the toast arranged on a platter, or spread it over the toast and broil it for a few seconds (as they do at St. John's). A third option is to pour the creamy sauce over the steamed cauliflower.

SERVES 4

Baked Asparagus with Poached Eggs and Fontina Cheese

Of these three suppers this is the quickest. It is elegant and pretty on the platter. I like to bake the asparagus in a handsome dish that I can bring right to the table.

Break off the ends of the asparagus and peel up to roughly two inches from the tips. Blanch in salted boiling water for about 4 minutes, depending on size. The spears should be slightly al dente, as they get a second cooking. Drain carefully.

    Preheat the oven to 400°F. Grease the bottom of a gratin dish with the olive oil.

    Arrange the asparagus with all tips pointing in the same direction. Drizzle olive oil over the asparagus and season with salt and pepper to taste.

    Crack the eggs on top of the asparagus so that they are evenly spaced. Season with salt and pepper. Scatter the cheese over the top. Bake for 7 minutes or until the eggs are set but still loose.

    Using a spatula, serve each person one quarter of the asparagus with one egg.

SERVES 4

1 pound thick asparagus

Splash of extra-virgin olive oil

Salt and freshly ground black pepper

4 large eggs

⅓ pound fontina cheese, grated

Classic Spinach Salad

This is a delicious, old-fashioned salad that is hearty enough to make a substantial meal along with one of the trio of supper dishes. Cook the bacon ahead of time so it will be cool enough to crumble. Hard-boil and grate the eggs ahead of time as well. Omit the egg if you are serving the asparagus recipe with eggs in it.

Place the spinach in a large salad bowl and chill it as you make the dressing.

    In a small bowl, combine the lemon juice, garlic, and salt and pepper to taste. Whisk and add the olive oil, whisk again.

    Toss the spinach with the dressing, adding the warm bacon fat, if desired. Add the bacon and eggs and toss again. Taste for seasoning and serve.

SERVES 4

2 to 3 pounds fresh spinach, washed, stemmed, and spun dry

3 tablespoons fresh lemon juice

1 clove garlic, minced

Salt and freshly ground black pepper

½ cup extra-virgin olive oil

4 slices bacon, cooked and crumbled (reserve a tablespoon of the bacon fat for the salad dressing)

2 hard-boiled eggs, grated

THE LIVELIEST
BIRTHDAY DINNER

Chilled Radishes with Sea Salt and Sweet Butter

· · · · ·

Provençal Beef Stew on Pappardelle Noodles

· · · · ·

Escarole Salad with Anchovy Vinaigrette

· · · · ·

Dark Chocolate Molten Cakes

My friend David Sheff, a contributing editor to *Playboy* and an author, was born on December 23; his birthday is cause to celebrate, even with all that goes on around that time of year. We often choose a good movie that plays late in the afternoon and return to my house for a party afterward. I get the dinner ready before we go out, then we come home, light a fire, heat up the meal, and eat for hours. It is a tradition now with old friends such as Armistead Maupin, and Sue Conley of Cowgirl Creamery. It is our liveliest party of the year.

The parties are always devised around a slow-cooked meat dish whose flavor benefits from having been made earlier in the day and then reheated just before we sit down. This year it is a *daube*, a deep rich beef stew, with a mysterious, subtle flavor that comes by way of the addition of a dried orange peel.

The meal starts the way many home-cooked French meals begin, with crisp radishes accompanied by sweet butter and good sea salt. They are a good choice here because they are not filling and pique the appetite for what is to come. After the rich stew and wide pappardelle noodles, escarole salad provides a crisp, slightly salty, pause to the meal before the insanely rich, warm, dark molten cakes. A candle will go into one of the cakes for the birthday boy.

PARTY PLAN

THE DAY BEFORE

- Dry the orange rind
- Make the stew

DAY OF THE PARTY

- Prepare and chill the radishes
- Wash the escarole and prepare dressing
- Prepare the cakes for baking

LAST MINUTE

- Reheat the stew
- Cook the noodles
- Bake the cakes

DECORATING IDEAS

Arrange a dozen or two pomegranates on a silver platter or in a large silver bowl. (You can usually find them at Christmastime in farmers' markets; if not, go for persimmons or red apples.) Stick small swags of holly and pine in the cracks between them. Put lots of white votive candles around the platter.

Another decorating idea, which I learned from an artist friend, is to gather 50 to 75 photographs of the guest of honor from over the years. Lay them on the dining table, stretch a sheet of light clear plastic over them and tape the edges under the table. Your guests will discover things about the birthday honoree they might never have imagined.

CHILLED RADISHES WITH SEA SALT AND SWEET BUTTER

Shown on page 205

Using the best radishes you can find, clean and remove the spindly stems, leaving on the crisp green part to grasp. Put them in ice water until ready to serve. Drain and serve in a dish with a small ramekin of sweet butter and another small ramekin of excellent quality sea salt.

PROVENÇAL BEEF STEW ON PAPPARDELLE NOODLES

FOR THE STEW

2 celery stalks or 2 green leaves of a leek stuffed with 3 sprigs fresh thyme

2 bay leaves

3-inch piece dried orange peel

6 to 8 parsley stems

4 to 5 pounds beef stew meat (chuck roast nicely marbled with some fat, do not use lean meat)

¾ pound thick-cut bacon

2 tablespoons extra-virgin olive oil

3 medium onions, thinly sliced

2 cloves garlic, flattened with the side of a knife

1 pound medium-sized carrots, peeled and cut into bite-sized chunks

Most regions in France have some sort of slow-cooked beef stew somewhere in their culinary memory. There is Burgundy's famous boeuf bourguignon, the carbonnades de boeuf à la flamande (beef and onions braised in beer from Flanders), but my favorite is the daube de boeuf using red wine and a bouquet garni with an orange rind tied in. Daube gets its name from the daubière, the covered casserole in which it is cooked.

A day before making the stew, I take a 1 inch by 3 inch piee of orange peel and lay it on the window sill to dry in the sun. It adds an imperceptible flavor to the stew, but it lurks there, under the surface, in the most pleasing way.

This dish actually improves by being reheated the day after its preparation.

Make a bouquet garni by tying together with kitchen twine the celery, thyme, bay leaves, orange peel, and parsley

Cut the beef into bite-sized pieces and set aside. Heat a large, heavy casserole and a large skillet over medium-high heat. Add half the bacon, along with 1 tablespoon of the olive oil to each. Fry the bacon until just barely crisp, so that some fat remains. Drain the bacon, cut it into 1 inch pieces and set it aside in a large bowl.

Working in batches with the two pans, add the beef and brown it on all sides; do not crowd. Add extra olive oil if necessary. Transfer the meat to the bowl with the bacon, seasoning each batch with salt and pepper. When all the meat is browned, pour off most of the fat from the pans and cook the onions, garlic, and carrots in the remaining juices and fat for about 10 minutes, stirring up the crispy bits from the bottom. Transfer the vegetables to a bowl.

Preheat the oven to 350°F.

Transfer the beef and bacon to the large casserole. Sprinkle the flour gently on each layer, so that most of the meat is dusted. Toss well with wooden spoons to incorporate, then let the flour brown for a few minutes over medium heat. Remove from the heat and add the vegetables.

Pour the wine in to cover the meat and the vegetables. Strain the porcini water through a coffee filter and add it, along with some of the beef stock, if necessary, to cover the meat. Stir in the tomato paste. Nestle the *bouquet garni* into the pieces of meat.

Cut a piece of parchment the size of the lid and press it on top of the stew. Place the casserole in the oven to cook for about 2 hours, removing the parchment and turning the meat every 45 minutes with a large spoon. Replace the parchment each time. When done, the meat should be very tender; you should able to be cut it with a spoon. It if is not tender enough, return it to the oven for another half hour or until juicy and tender.

Meanwhile heat the butter in a large skillet and sauté the mushrooms until their water is given off and reabsorbed, 10 to 15 minutes.

When the stew is done, remove the parchment and the *bouquet garni*. Stir in both types of mushrooms. (The stew can be made ahead of time to this point, cooled to room temperature, and refrigerated. A couple of hours before serving, remove the stew from the refrigerator and bring to room temperature.)

Return the stew to the oven and heat until it is hot and bubbling, about 15 minutes. Remove it from the oven and sprinkle the chopped parsley on top.

Meanwhile, cook the noodles according to the directions on the package. Drain, and toss them with enough butter to make them slippery, about 3 tablespoons. Serve in a warm serving bowl alongside the beef stew, scattering the parsley on top.

SERVES 8 TO 10

Salt and freshly ground black pepper

Handful of flour

1 to 1½ bottles dry red wine

4 grams dried porcini mushroom, soaked in a cup of hot water

2 cups beef stock, preferably homemade or low-sodium, as needed

3 tablespoons tomato paste

2 tablespoons unsalted butter

2 pounds fresh brown or wild mushrooms, cleaned and sliced

1 cup chopped flat-leaf parsley

FOR THE NOODLES

1 pound pappardelle noodles

3 tablespoons unsalted butter

Escarole Salad with Anchovy Vinaigrette

FOR THE DRESSING

2 medium-sized cloves garlic, minced

¼ teaspoon salt

Freshly ground black pepper

4 to 6 anchovy fillets, chopped

3 tablespoons fresh lemon juice

⅓ to ½ cup extra-virgin olive oil

3 to 4 medium bunches escarole, tough outer leaves discarded, washed and dried

Escarole is a smooth chicory with broad, pale green leaves. It is grown widely in France, around the Mediterranean, and in California. Often confused with romaine lettuce, escarole has its own mildly bitter distinction and stands up nicely to an anchovy dressing.

TO MAKE THE DRESSING

Using a mortar and pestle, combine the garlic, salt, and pepper to taste. Add the anchovies and pound again. Whisk in the lemon juice, add the olive oil, and whisk again. Alternatively, place the garlic, salt, pepper, and anchovies in the bowl of a food processor, then add the lemon juice and olive oil and pulse until combined.

Tear the escarole just before serving as the torn tips tend to brown with exposure to air. Place them in a salad bowl to chill in the refrigerator as you make the dressing.

Toss the escarole with the dressing, using your hands to make sure that all the leaves are coated.

SERVES 8

Mortar and Pestle

No good cook can live without one or two. Using a mortar and pestle for sauces makes all the difference in the world. All recipes for sauces in this book are given with this in mind. I can always tell when a cook takes a shortcut and uses a food processor—it makes the sauce too pureed, too uniform, and not as tasty.

Dark Chocolate Molten Cakes

These warm, soft-centered chocolate cakes are so romantic and pleasing. But best of all, they are really easy. The only special ingredient you need is excellent quality chocolate, such as E. Guittard or Valrhona. You will also need individual soufflé dishes. These dishes can be filled and set on a baking sheet up to a few hours before baking. Then, pop them in the oven just before dessert time.

This recipe is adapted from a recipe from the old Russian Tea Room in New York City (Andrew Garrison Shotts, chef).

In a double boiler (or in a bowl set tightly over a pot of simmering water), melt the butter with the chocolate, stirring constantly until all the chocolate has melted. Remove from the heat and allow to cool for about 30 minutes. You can place the bowl in the refrigerator briefly, but do not let the chocolate harden.

Preheat the oven to 400°F. Grease six 6-ounce individual soufflé dishes and place them on a baking sheet.

Combine the flour and sugar in a medium-sized bowl. Whisk in the eggs until well blended and there are no visible lumps. Whisk in the cooled chocolate mixture until combined completely. Divide the batter evenly among the soufflé dishes, they should be two thirds full. (The recipe can be made in advance up to this point and refrigerated for up to 6 hours. Bring to room temperature before baking.)

Bake on the middle rack of the oven for 10 to 12 minutes. The centers will be slightly fluid at 10 minutes, and a little more cakelike if baked for 12 minutes.

Serve in the soufflé dishes, or invert the cakes onto plates. Serve with sweetened whipped cream on the side or on top, or in a separate bowl for guests to help themselves.

FOR THE CAKE

8 tablespoons (1 stick) unsalted butter

10 ounces E. Guittard or other excellent-quality dark chocolate, broken into chunks

⅓ cup plus 2 tablespoons all-purpose flour

¼ cup sugar

4 large eggs, beaten

FOR THE TOPPING (optional)

Sweetened whipped cream or crème fraîche

A Post-Performance Party

Marinated Jicama, Roasted Almonds, Assorted Olives,
Salt-and-Vinegar Chips

. . . . .

Roasted Asian-Spiced Pork Ribs

. . . . .

Mississippi-Style Corn Bread
(PAGE 144)

. . . . .

Fennel, Blood Orange, and Arugula Salad

. . . . .

Radicchio Salad with Roasted Walnuts and Parmesan

. . . . .

Coffee Crunch Cake

A while ago, David Sedaris, the wryly irreverent humorist, was giving a reading in San Francisco. My friend Steven Barclay, an agent, asked if I would have a little dinner party for David and another client, Billy Collins, former poet laureate, also reading in the city that night. I was thrilled at the prospect and realized that I needed a special menu for this group of literary lions that now included author Michael Ondaatje and his wife, author Linda Spaulding, and Alice Waters, who was going to the Collins reading.

Since the pre-party situation was not ideal (I would be at the reading) I needed a menu that would be easy on my nervous system and up to snuff for the snazzy guests I was so lucky to be cooking for. David had exhibited a fondness for meat and cake, and I heard that Billy liked gin. Since Michael and Linda were new to the area, I wanted something typically San Franciscan for them.

I decided on spareribs, as they hold up surprisingly well when cooked earlier and gently reheated, and corn bread has an affinity for ribs. Two salads—radicchio with roasted walnuts, and blood orange and fennel—would be crunchy and colorful. There was no deliberation about the dessert, it would be the old-fashioned coffee crunch cake first made at Blum's, the long-gone San Francisco confection haunt. To be honest, I was delighted to be serving a meal featuring red meat, cigarettes, hard liquor, and lots of sugar! The dinner was a huge hit—the ultimate simple soirée.

PARTY PLAN

THE DAY BEFORE

- Make the spice rub and rub the ribs with it
- Make the cake
- Make the crunch and store in an airtight container

DAY OF THE PARTY

- Prepare and cook the ribs
- Make the dressings for the salads
- Assemble the salads
- Make the corn bread
- Roast the nuts

LAST MINUTE

- Reheat the ribs
- Assemble and dress both salads
- Assemble the cake, whip the cream, and frost it

DECORATING IDEAS

I love to write out a menu and attach it to the refrigerator door. It helps me, and the guests always seem to be interested in what is being served. I had orchids clustered around the room and lots and lots of candles. Alice Waters brought a copper bowl filled with tangerines, so we placed them in the center of the table.

Marinated Jicama

1 large jicama, peeled and cut into 1-inch rounds

3 tablespoons fresh lime juice

Pinch of salt

Pinch of fresh chile powder

This simple salad is served as street food in Oaxaca, Mexico. It's cooling and crunchy first, and ends with a little heat from the chile powder.

Toss the jicama with the lime juice and salt. Arrange in a bowl and sprinkle the chile powder over the top. Add extra salt, if necessary.

SERVES 6 TO 8

Fennel, Blood Orange, and Arugula Salad

FOR THE DRESSING

3 tablespoons sherry vinegar

2 shallots, minced

Salt and freshly ground black pepper

½ cup extra-virgin olive oil

FOR THE SALAD

3 to 4 medium heads fennel, tough outer leaves discarded

4 to 6 blood oranges, peeled

A few handfuls of arugula leaves, washed and dried

Niçoise olives, for garnish

The beauty of this salad lies in the crimson color of the blood oranges. If blood oranges are unavailable, you might use tangerine sections or orange slices.

TO MAKE THE DRESSING
In a small bowl combine the vinegar with the shallots and salt and pepper to taste. Allow it to macerate for a few minutes then whisk in the olive oil.

TO MAKE THE SALAD
Cut the fennel in half lengthwise, removing the core. Cut the fennel into thin strips and place in a salad bowl. Cut the oranges into slices, removing any pith and stray pits, or cut out sections of the fruit by slicing on either side of the membranes and letting the clean pieces of orange fall out. Add the orange slices to the bowl and toss gently with the dressing and the arugula leaves. Sprinkle the olives on top.

SERVES 6 TO 8

Roasted Asian-Spiced Pork Ribs

These ribs, seasoned with a delightfully haunting rub, can be roasted at a low temperature for about 3 hours and served as is, or they can be cooked for about 2½ hours in the oven and finished on the grill. Either way, they are remarkable. They can be made ahead of time and reheated. This perfect party dish is from chef Steve Johnson of Cambridge.

TO MAKE THE RUB

Blend all of the rub ingredients in a food processor, blender, or with a mortar and pestle until grainy. Apply liberally to the ribs and rub into both sides. Let the ribs stand for at least 1 hour before cooking.

TO MAKE THE SAUCE

In a small bowl, stir together all the sauce ingredients. Set aside.

TO PREPARE THE RIBS

Preheat the oven to 300°F.

Place the rib slabs on baking sheets, meaty side up and bake, without turning for 2½ to 3 hours. Brush with the sauce during the last half hour of cooking. It is a good idea to rotate the pans, and if using two baking sheets, switch their position in the oven every 30 minutes or so.

A good test for doneness is to pick the ribs up in the middle with tongs. The cartilage and fat will have broken down and they are done when the ends of the ribs flop. (I always cut down the center of the ribs and taste one rib; if it is falling-off-the-bone-tender, remove them from the oven.)

TO SERVE

Brush the ribs with the sauce and place them meaty side down and cut them into 1- or 2-rib servings (with a cleaver or with poultry shears). Arrange them on a large serving platter, and brush again with the sauce. Scatter the sesame seeds and a few sprigs of cilantro over the top.

SERVES 6 TO 8

FOR THE RUB

3 tablespoons coriander seeds, or ground coriander

1 tablespoon five-spice powder

2 tablespoons star anise, whole

1 tablespoon fennel seed

1 tablespoon ground ginger

½ teaspoon cayenne pepper

1 teaspoon crushed red pepper flakes

1 teaspoon cinnamon

1 teaspoon freshly ground black pepper

2 tablespoons salt

¼ cup brown sugar

FOR THE BASTING SAUCE

¼ cup toasted sesame seed oil

2 tablespoons minced garlic

2 tablespoons minced ginger

¼ cup white wine

Juice of 1 orange

¼ cup soy sauce

3 whole star anise

1 teaspoon crushed red pepper flakes

FOR THE RIBS

6 to 8 pounds Chinese–style pork ribs (sometimes called St. Louis ribs)

FOR GARNISH

Toasted sesame seeds

Cilantro sprigs

Radicchio Salad with Roasted Walnuts and Parmesan

5 to 6 heads radicchio (depending upon size and tightness of heads)

2 tablespoons balsamic vinegar

1 tablespoon red wine vinegar

Sea salt

1 large shallot, minced

5 ounces (about 1 cup) walnuts

½ cup extra-virgin olive oil

2 to 3 ounces Parmesan cheese

There are so many varieties of radicchio at farmers' markets these days. Either go for the most common rossa Chiogia (tight, red and white cabbage-shaped head) or the long, similarly colored variety, rossa di Treviso. With either of these, separate the leaves, soak them well in a few changes of cold water, then dry on kitchen towels. Roll up the leaves in clean dry towels and refrigerate until ready to dress. The sweetness of the balsamic addresses the bitterness of the radicchio.

Rinse the radicchio and spin dry. Store in the refrigerator until ready to use.

Place the vinegars, salt, and shallot in a small bowl and set aside to macerate.

Place a medium-sized heavy skillet over medium-high heat. When the pan is hot, add the walnuts and roast them, shaking the pan or stirring them for a few minutes, or until you start to smell a nutty aroma. Transfer the nuts to a cutting board and let them cool. Chop coarsely and set aside.

Transfer the radicchio to a large salad bowl, breaking up the leaves with your fingers. Add the walnuts. Whisk the olive oil into the vinegar mixture. Pour the dressing over the radicchio and toss. Shave the cheese on top.

SERVES 6 TO 8

COFFEE CRUNCH CAKE

This cake, created by Marion Cunningham and her daughter Katherine, by way of Blum's Restaurant, is the best present you could possibly give your guests. If you make it in stages, starting the day before your party, it will be less daunting. It isn't hard, it just needs to be made calmly, stage by stage. When you have made it once, it will become your special celebration cake.

Some hints: To make a successful cake, you must have a candy thermometer for the coffee crunch. It's a good idea to make the crunch first, then make the cake at least 4 hours before you plan to frost it. You can make both a day ahead, then you just have to make the easy whipped cream frosting at the last minute. Do not frost the cake more than an hour before serving.

TO MAKE THE COFFEE CRUNCH

Lightly oil a baking sheet.

Combine the sugar, coffee, and corn syrup in a heavy-bottomed, 4-quart saucepan (the mixture becomes very foamy after the baking soda is added and rises high in the pan) and bring to a boil. Cook almost to the hard-crack stage (285°F on a candy thermometer), approximately 6 to 7 minutes. The mixture will be slightly smoky with a strong aroma of coffee as it cooks.

Remove the pan from the heat and count to 10. Sprinkle on the baking soda, making sure to distribute it as evenly as possible, so there are no clumps visible. Whisk just enough to distribute the soda throughout. Be careful, the mixture is very hot and will foam up high, looking like golden lava as it bubbles up. When it stops rising and foaming (after a minute or two) immediately pour it onto the baking sheet. Spread it out with a spatula, and let sit until it has cooled and hardened.

Using a small hammer, break the coffee crunch into irregular ¼- to ½-inch-pieces, you don't want crumbs. If you do get some, save them for the in-between layer. Store in an airtight container until ready to use. (You can make the coffee crunch up to two days ahead of time. If the weather is humid, the brickle will become moist, don't worry, just break up the clumps.)

(Continued)

FOR THE COFFEE CRUNCH

Vegetable oil for oiling the baking sheet

1½ cups sugar

¼ cup strong coffee

¼ cup light corn syrup

1 tablespoon baking soda, sifted after measuring

FOR THE CAKE

8 large egg whites

1½ cups sugar

2¼ cups cake flour

1 tablespoon baking powder

1 teaspoon salt

½ cup vegetable oil

6 large egg yolks

3/4 cup water

2 teaspoons lemon zest, grated

1 tablespoon vanilla extract

FOR THE FROSTING

3 cups (1½ pints) heavy whipping cream

2 teaspoons vanilla extract

½ cup confectioners' sugar

1 tablespoon instant coffee, such as Medalia D'Oro

TO MAKE THE CAKE

Preheat oven to 350°F.

Using an electric mixer, beat the egg whites in a large mixing bowl until they begin to foam. Slowly add ¾ cup of the sugar, and continue beating until the whites are stiff but still moist. Transfer to a bowl and set aside.

Sift together the flour, the remaining ¾ cup sugar, the baking powder, and the salt in a small mixing bowl. Place the oil, egg yolks, ¾ cup water, lemon zest, and vanilla in a large bowl and beat with an electric mixer until completely smooth. Add the flour mixture and stir to combine well.

Gently fold one third of the beaten whites into the batter. Once incorporated, drop the remaining whites onto the batter and fold them in. Pour the batter into an ungreased 10-inch tube pan, and smooth the top with a rubber spatula.

Bake in the top half of the oven for 80 to 90 minutes, or until a wooden skewer inserted in the cake comes out clean. Remove from the oven and immediately invert the pan onto the neck of a wine bottle until it is completely cool. Turn the pan right side up and use a knife to go around the side of the pan to loosen the cake, push the center up and remove the cake from the pan. When done, wrap in plastic wrap until ready to frost—it will keep for a day.

TO MAKE THE FROSTING

Combine the cream and vanilla in a deep bowl. Sift the confectioners' sugar and instant coffee together twice, then add to the cream and vanilla. Using a whisk, rotary, or electric beater, whip the cream until soft peaks form. It must be stiff enough to spread.

TO ASSEMBLE

Split the cake into 2 equal layers. Using a spatula, frost the bottom layer and sprinkle it with the coffee crunch. Place the second cake layer on top, frost it, and sprinkle the top and the side of the cake generously with the coffee crunch.

SERVES 10

ACKNOWLEDGMENTS

THANK YOU

To Christopher Hirsheimer for making my food look more beautiful than I could have imagined; for endless trips to Paris and San Francisco; and for all the help with recipes. To Diane Johnson for her welcoming friendship in Paris and for the stunning foreword.

To Carole Bidnick, my dedicated and hardworking agent. To Leslie Stoker, my kind, imaginative publisher at STC. To Julie Stillman, my thorough, creative editor. To Eleanor Betino, my confidante and advisor.

To Marti and Jack Cowden, my stepparents, to whom I am grateful for having a second chance. Ron and Madeline Shalita for patiently trying recipes. To Tony Knickerbocker, my wonderful younger brother, and the equally wonderful Mary Lawler.

To Alice Waters for her inspiration and company in the kitchen and at the table. To Randal Breski—for making my life fuller and more amusing. To David Tanis for encouragement in the kitchen. To Tony Oltranti and Bob Carrau for making simple soirées simple and fun. To Niloufer and David King for tasting. To Angelo for integrating his adventuresome ways with food into his friendships. To Cal Ferris for her love and generosity.

To Richard Overstreet and Agnes Montenay for making me feel at home in Paris. Daniel LeClercq for his always direct and amusing French point of view. Inez Casalderry for her recipes for orange carpaccio and for île flottante. To Garth Bixler for testing and discussing many menus and recipes. To Steven Barclay for friendship in Paris and for his unending generosity. To Barbara Barclay for her crispy creamy chocolate cookies. To Susie and Mark Buell for warm hospitality and tables for simple soirées.

To Fletcher for making everything peacefully beautiful. To Kathleen and Ed Weber for recipe testing. To Kay and Don Baumhefner. To Daryl Nelson for enormous generosity. To Terry Gamble my dear friend and model to whom I write, and to her writing group, Phyllis Florin, Sheri Cooper Bounds, and Suzanne Lewis for their help with the book. To Davia for sound and collaboration and Valerie for inspired movement.

To the annual birthday party group: David Sheff; Karen Barbour for her artful ways; Armistead Maupin for his unmistakable loveable laugh; Susan Andrews for testing recipes and walking; Buddy Rhodes, my favorite dinner partner; Sue Conley for remarkable cheesemaking accomplishments; and Nan Haynes for stories.

To Paula Wolfert for her unerring helpfulness. To Cristina Salas Porras for the Mexican fiesta advice. To Marion Cunningham for meeting me for dinner. To Steve Johnson for help with meat and rubs. To Sue Murphy for her humor. To Sue Moore for her delicate palate and her recipe for cardamom cookies.

To Shila Marie Joseph who keeps my life together in Paris. To my Parisian friends in food and politics: Constance Borde and Sheila Malovany-Chevallier. To Georgeanne Brennan for her work on French food and table decorating ideas. To Beverly Mills for her artistic decorating. To Alex Miles, my long-lost friend, for research in France. To Pierre Freau for tracking down Gnafron, and Shannon Latta for helping. And finally to my dear friends Jillian Clark, Mary Estrin, Laurel Gonsalves, Karina Hickey, Lindita Klein, Ingrid Kornspan, and Flicka McGurrin, for all of the simple soirées over the years.

CONVERSION CHARTS

WEIGHT EQUIVALENTS

The metric weights given in this chart are not exact equivalents, but have been rounded up or down slightly to make measuring easier.

AVOIRDUPOIS	METRIC
¼ oz	7 g
½ oz	15 g
1 oz	30 g
2 oz	60 g
3 oz	90 g
4 oz	115 g
5 oz	150 g
6 oz	175 g
7 oz	200 g
8 oz (½ lb)	225 g
9 oz	250 g
10 oz	300 g
11 oz	325 g
12 oz	350 g
13 oz	375 g
14 oz	400 g
15 oz	425 g
16 oz (1 lb)	450 g
1½ lb	750 g
2 lb	900 g
2¼ lb	1 kg
3 lb	1.4 kg
4 lb	1.8 kg

VOLUME EQUIVALENTS

These are not exact equivalents for American cups and spoons, but have been rounded up or down slightly to make measuring easier.

AMERICAN	METRIC	IMPERIAL
¼ t	1.2 ml	
½ t	2.5 ml	
1 t	5.0 ml	
½ T (1.5 t)	7.5 ml	
1 T (3 t)	15 ml	
¼ cup (4 T)	60 ml	2 fl oz
⅓ cup (5 T)	75 ml	2½ fl oz
½ cup (8 T)	125 ml	4 fl oz
⅔ cup (10 T)	150 ml	5 fl oz
¾ cup (12 T)	175 ml	6 fl oz
1 cup (16 T)	250 ml	8 fl oz
1¼ cups	300 ml	10 fl oz (½ pt)
1½ cups	350 ml	12 fl oz
2 cups (1 pint)	500 ml	16 fl oz
2½ cups	625 ml	20 fl oz (1 pint)
1 quart	1 liter	32 fl oz

OVEN TEMPERATURE EQUIVALENTS

OVEN MARK	F	C	GAS
Very cool	250–275	130–140	½–1
Cool	300	150	2
Warm	325	170	3
Moderate	350	180	4
Moderately hot	375	190	5
	400	200	6
Hot	425	220	7
	450	230	8
Very hot	475	250	9

SOURCES

Duck legs
www.dartagnan.com
www.grimaud.com

Fresh black truffles
www.plantin.com

Excellent quality pork, beef, and lamb
www.nimanranch.com

Excellent artisan cheeses
www.cowgirlcreamery.com
www.artisanalcheese.com

Topnotch chocolate
www.eguittard.com

Fennel pollen
www.fennelpollen.com

Spanish pimenton
www.spanishtable.com

Wild Pacific salmon
www.capecleare.com
www.ecofish.com

Party-planning advice
www.simple-soirees.com

INDEX

(Page numbers in **bold** denote photographs)

To the men in San Francisco

and Paris with whom I have

cooked and shared innumerable

exquisite simple soirées:

RANDAL and DAVID

STEVEN and GARTH

BOB and TONY

Published in 2005 by
Stewart, Tabori & Chang
115 West 18th Street
New York, NY 10011
www.abramsbooks.com

Library of Congress Cataloging-in-Publication Data

Knickerbocker, Peggy
    Simple soirées : seasonal menus for sensational dinner parties / Peggy Knickerbocker ; foreword by Diane Johnson ; photographs by Christopher Hirsheimer.
        p. cm.
    ISBN 1-58479-460-7
1. Dinners and dining. 2. Entertaining. 3. Menus. I. Title.

    TX737.K65 2005
    642'.4—dc22   2005044210

Edited by Julie Stillman
Designed by Susi Oberhelman
Graphic Production by Jane Searle

The text of this book was composed in the Seria Family

Printed in Thailand

10 9 8 7 6 5 4 3 2

Stewart, Tabori & Chang is a Subsidiary of

LA MARTINIÈRE
GROUPE